Victoria –
My partner in crime!
I love you for!
Thank you for be
such a friend
when I needed
you.

What I Love About You...

My Appreciation For Women

Kaiserrific ...

You are truly my
an inspiration my
friend .

Kaiserrific

09-11-2015

Kaiserrific

DISCLAIMER

This book is strictly for entertainment purposes. Everything that was written for this book was solely created for the enjoyment of the reader. All names, characters, businesses, places, events and incidents are either the products of the author's imagination and or used in a fictitious manner. Any resemblance to actual persons, living or dead, or actual events is purely coincidental. I apologize in advance for anything that I've written that is found to be highly offensive or personal.

Kaiserrific

What I Love About You... *My Appreciation For Women* is a registered trademark and is published by Kaiserrific.

All poems originally written by
Kaiserrific

Edited by
Cynthia C. Jowers & Kaiserrific

Managed by
Belle Be for Be Artist Entertainment

Book cover designed by
Anthony Stewart

Photo of Kaiserrific taken by
Kim Lambert for PT Personal Touch Photography & Creations

All quotes from famous women were taken from www.brainyquote.com

Quote #19 taken from X Blu Rayne's Words by Blu

Poet Lightning Quote courtesy of Poet Lightning

ISBN-13: 978-1506190389

PRINTED IN THE UNITED STATES OF AMERICA

Dedication

To all women, you have value and worth. You all are so special and important…

Acknowledgments

First I want to thank God for blessing me with the gift to write this beautiful book. Through all I have been through as I prepared this book God see to it that it would be finished. God is real and I am witnessed to that. Again as always I thank you...

I want to thank my beautiful mother, Roslind Kaiser because without her influence and love I wouldn't be here. She had shown me all my life was passed down to me. I was able to write freely from my heart. She's the woman that taught me to read or write before I ever enter into a classroom. My biggest supporter of what I did from the very beginning that had my back when I didn't have anyone else. Momma you are truly my biggest influence. I love you...

I want to acknowledge my beautiful grandmother the late Mrs. Annie Mae Kaiser; I know it's been a long time since she left us from this world. She left such an inspiring influence in my life. Our talks and her explaining things to me to where I can understand will always be cherished. Gone but never forgotten.

Kaiserrific

To my son Kemonee Kaiser a.k.a. Kid Kaiserrific, I want to say thank you for being an influence in my life to keep moving forward so that I can show these examples of what hard work pays off. You are growing to be a fine young man and I am so proud of you. I do all of this for you so you can know that your dad wasn't doing anything that he shouldn't have been doing. I love you son...

I want to thank my family for your continuous support. You deeply appreciated.

My manager and my long time friend Belle Be within the past year, you and I both have witnessed changes within our lives both good and bad. Through it all we stuck it out and remain on top in the end throughout all of this. During a time when we only had each other to lift the other up and encourage each other to move forward. I see we both are doing well now and overcome the hump. Thank you for building this new empire with Be Artist Ent. I see great things developing from this and again we will go to the top! I love you and I most definitely thank you for bringing back a part of me that was falling by the waste side but you saved me before it was too late.

My family at Be Artist Entertainment (Be Artist Ent.). You all are amazing! I know that we all are in the beginning stages but I see the future of where we all are going. I can say it's beyond anything I have ever seen. Let's continue to love and support each other through this struggle and come out on top. I love you all…

Aja LaStarr, Belle Be, LaVita Bell, LaShawn Glass, Mea Hampton, Michelle L. Artist, Poet Lightning, Poet Janet Dawson, Raye Cole, Shayla Muhammad, Shea Brown, Sistah Taraji, Talisha Mallory, X Blu Rayne, Victoria Spence, truly from the bottom of my heart I want to say thank you. Without each one of you taking me in and influencing me one way or another. You all have made Kaiserrific who I am today. I thank each one of you for the love and inspiration for my journey.

To the family of Pamela Champion, I want to say thank you for being such a loving family. I remember the days that I got to be with you all at the concert on the landing and at Traci's play in

Springfield. Pam meant a lot to me as she did to all of you. She was truly a great inspiration to me that kept me together. I am truly grateful to have known such a wonderful person. I miss her dearly and she remains in my thoughts.

Anthony Stewart also known as The Mixologist, the man that has feed me throughout the last few years these wonderful dishes thank you for the help you put in to create this beautiful book cover. I appreciate all the encouraging things you have said in the past and current. I have taken everything you have said and applied it to everything that I do in my everyday life. You are a true friend and that what true friends have done for me. Thank you again.

Cynthia C. Jowers, my sister from another mother and my close friend thank you for everything. Whenever we are around each other you are always showing me another side to life. You are one of the few people in my life that will not allow me to fail in anything that I do. I appreciate everything that you have done for me in the time that we've known each other. Your love and time together will always be appreciated. Thank you…

Kathy (Lynn) Gray, I want to say a very special thank you for being a very important part of my life. I was 15 when I first met you at Normandy and I have always thought of you as a second mother to me. It was you that kept me believing in all of my dreams. Because like some of my other teachers you was concerned about us and got involved in our lives when you didn't have to. You prepared us for what we were about to face in the real world. I know you may say that was your job but to me that was all love. Thank you for being such a major influence on my life. You being in my life kept me in high school for all of those four years.

Jo Lena Johnson, thank you for continuing to be such an inspiration. This is my first books that you will get to enjoy without non-excessive language. I appreciate all of our talks. Thank you and God Bless.

Kim and Jason, what can I say I gain new friends and hanging with you both has been the best. I keep a laugh everytime that I am with you both. You all do some wonderful pictures and I am glad to have you all around to be a part of this project.

Poet Janet Dawson, thank you for being there. I miss you dearly. You played a major role to my artistry. We bonded the moment we started talking. You had a strong influence on this book. I look forward to us working together again soon.

M'Reld Green, you are truly an inspiration to me. Whenever you come to town and perform and I get a chance to see you. I am left with such inspiration. I thank you for having the opportunity of knowing you and getting to see you perform.

Nicole Humphries a.k.a Poetic Dreams, thank you for being such a wonderful friend. God lead me into your direction when I called you many of times when I was working on this book. I want to say thank you for the times you would listen to and your critiques. Friends for life and that's real. Again thank you.

Kim Edwards a.k.a Sensations of the Truth, I truly want to say thank you for the support you have shown me during the short time of knowing each other. The fire you contain in your poetry is so on point and I am definitely inspired by you.

Look forward to working with you in the near future on future projects.

I want to say thank you to all my friends who stuck with me during the times that I was writing the poems to this book. Being at my side when I had the vision of this book coming together and your support truly means a lot to me. Again thank you.

AD, Cordeyell, Corey, Fred, Kelvin, Monties Prolyric, and Wildmann I want to thank my brothas for guiding and school through this journey. You all play major contributions to me bringing the artistic side of Kaiserrific.

I specially want to thank all the marketers, promoters, and venues that have allowed me to come out and perform at their events in the past. If it wasn't for you all allowing me to be a part of your events Kaiserrific would not be known or heard of without you all. Again I want to say thank you from the bottom of my heart. You all have made such a difference in my life. I vow to continue supporting you all as you all have supported me. Thank you.

Last and never least I want to thank everyone that has ever came out to see me perform, listened to my interviews, showed me the upmost support and has bought copies of my books. I truly thank you and much love to you for everything. You the readers/audience have made such a huge difference in my life that allows me to continue to go forward and write more. From the bottom of my heart, I want to say thank you.

Table Of Contents

What I Love About You - *Reason Five* **95**

What I Love About You - *Reason Six* **147**

What I Love About You - *Reason Seven* ... 174

What I Love About You - *Reason Eight* 196

Introduction

In February of 2014 I was challenged by a friend to write a poem to say something positive and uplifting to women. So with concentrated thoughts I wrote a poem called *WHAT I LOVE ABOUT YOU*. The poem circles around about how I loved the attributes of women portrayal in our world. So when the poem was finally posted on social media, the feedback went to the roof. Women from everywhere told me how much they truly enjoyed this poem. From there on, I wanted to create a poetry book that shows women that I appreciate and love them for just being exactly who they are…women

In creating this poetry book I went a lot deeper and began brainstorming about where my appreciation for women came from. It came to me to where it all began, with the woman that showed me love from the very start was my mom. She is the first woman that ever loved and appreciated me for who I was. Of course she did it because I was her child but because she did it from the heart.

Growing up my mother was a great teacher when it came to being loyal to women. She showed that women love to feel appreciated as well as understood at the same time nurtured. With how some men treatment of women has been portrayed through all the media outlets these last several years; I wanted to take a detour and do something different.

It was a pleasure writing this book creating poetry that will appreciate women of all ages. During my time as I wrote the poems to this book, some of the pieces helped me with unhealed wounds that I have kept inside for so long. It was my way of letting go of past hurt and pain that was stored in my heart from many years ago.

So in creating this book I took the time to give special appreciation to the women that made very important impact on my life. Starting with my mother who was the first leading up to such people like Maya Angelou and Ruby Dee. Along with some of my close friends who were there with me when I decided to become a spoken word poet. I owe each one of these ladies much appreciation to the birth of Kaiserrific.

In addition to my appreciation to those ladies, I wanted to give more appreciation to every woman. I decided to get off into letting the ladies know that there is a man out that sees their pain and their hurt. I may not exactly know what they have dealt with but do know that they are not forgotten. During writing some of the pieces for this book I had several breakdowns to where I began involving some of my feelings that I haven't deal with in years. I realized that this book was talking to me as well. Acknowledging my growth from where I started and to end all rumored thoughts that were probably made up about me and feelings towards women.

I hope that expectations from what I'm guessing are that you will not want to put this book down. I believe that you will shed a tear or two and will be shocked that this is coming from a man. Ladies, you all hold a very important place to my heart. In my opinion, without you all wouldn't be me.

I, Kaiserrific, the author of this book would love to extend my thanks for your love and inspiration to this book. I hope that you all enjoy reading this book as much as I did writing it. Love, peace, and Kaiserrific…. Enjoy *WHAT I LOVE ABOUT YOU, My Appreciation For Women*!

What I Love About You...

Reason Number One

"Loving oneself isn't hard, when you understand who and what 'yourself' is. It has nothing to do with the shape of your face, the size of your eyes, the length of your hair or the quality of your clothes. It's so beyond all of those things and it's what gives life to everything about you. Your own self is such a treasure."- Phylicia Rashād

Hello

Hello beautiful
Hello queen
Hello my future
Hello my new destiny
Hello my life partner
Hello to my completion

Hmmmm

I notice your worth
I see your value
You hold a very important place to my world
And so what if you not important to that other
person
You're important to me and that what matters

Hello my sweetheart
Hello dear one closest to my heart
Hello to the woman who shares my ending and is
always my start
Hello woman of worth whom I never want to
part
Hello to you being my galaxies that touches my
stars
You may not feel the importance of you in my
world

Kaiserrific

You keep my spirits warm as we walk through a
world that remains cold
So hello baby…

That's how important you are to me, baby
Without any of you ladies it wouldn't be no me
This is why you all are important

Hello to the woman that suffers from a broken
heart
Hello to the woman that feels that she is not
noticed
Hello to the woman that desires attention
Hello to the woman that wants to be pampered

Hello to the woman that walks with low self
esteem about herself
Hello to the woman who feels like she's so alone
Hello to the woman that feels that she can't find
a good man, hello
Hello to the woman who has lost all confidence
in who she is as a woman
Hello to the woman that feels that she has no
place in the world
Hello
Hello

Kaiserrific

Hello, I love your smile
I love your personality
I love your character
I love your humor
I enjoy your conversation
I appreciate your time
I love being loved by you
Thank you for being an important part of our
lives
When no one else doesn't acknowledges your
worth like I do

Hello is WHAT I LOVE ABOUT YOU…

Existence, Worth, And Value Of A Woman

Ladies, I have questions for you,
Once you know the answers you'll know where I
am taking you
But first let me ask you ladies this,
Do you love you?
Do you know your own worth?
Did you know that you have value?
Do you know how much your existence means?
Do you know that you play an important role in
any man's life?
It's more to you than being someone's sex slave
and somebody's wife?

Always remember that you are the queen of your
castle
You're the women that fights so many wars as
you all deal with other battles
You got the power to nurture one pains and
hassles
That's why you are always placed above the rest
Because not only are you simply beautiful but
you are simply the best

Kaiserrific

Remember if you ladies so happen to be
struggling with a bill or two,
Do you need some money to help out with that
bill?
Call us and we will cover you
If you or the children gets hungry, in need of
something to eat
Call us and we will bring you all those delicious
treats
We know that times get hard for all of us
And during these times where we must have each
other back
Instead of us being divided amongst the pack

Do you know who you truly are?
Did you see pass the foundation of who you
really are?
Pass the hair, the makeup, and the curves
Beyond the image that movies and music videos
portray you out to be
And realize that you are a true queens, mothers,
wives, and friend
Through my eyes you all are my movie stars?
Capturing the real identity of the woman you
were born to be
Beautiful woman where did you come from?
Did you come from here or far?

Kaiserrific

Did you know that women before your time were
placed on a throne?
Not only did these powerful women held the title
but held our crown
Receiving from us the best treatment in all of the
world
Something that men should have already
practiced and condone
These are the practices that man must know
never gets old
Did you know that we men are supposed to open
your doors?
We men are to go pull up the car so we can open
the door when you're leaving out,
So you wouldn't have to take a far walk to the
car
And as the only women in our life,
We men are supposed to give you A Plus
treatment made not for a girlfriend but for a wife
Women did you know we suppose to come
knock on your door
Instead of us sitting in the car and honking the
horn
'Cause I wouldn't want you to get the
assumption that we are calling you ladies hoes
When it comes to how us men refer to you
wonderful woman

Kaiserrific

Bitch
Hoe
Slut
Ratchet
Thot
Are not the terms we use in our vocabulary,
But Queen
My Future
My Better Half
Wife
Best Friend
Are words that we call and describe you from the
beginning to the very end

But remember your worth
Your value to life
How important you all are in our lives
Your history and role in this society
Remember your morals
We are with you as you all deal with the struggle
and the fight

*To all real and true women in the world...thank
you!*

Idea Woman

Ideally speaking, she was made for me
Made for all of my wants and has been there for
all of my needs
Appeared early on in my life, in my dreams
To help me let go of my past hurt as she builds
up my self esteem
This beautiful idea woman
Ideally, she is the main ingredient of my life
made for just me

A woman that I've asked for many times in every
last one of my prayers
An idea woman that can share every last one of
my wildest dreams
Ideally, the perfect soulmate that God has created
just for me
One woman that is beyond what any man has
ever dreamed
My idea woman
Ideally, a woman that was created in my sleep
made for just me

Maybe she wasn't the right woman for him
But designed for me to finish and complete my
missing pieces,

Pieces to my unique puzzle made specifically for
me
The prototype of my idea woman
Ideally, the complete blueprint designed made
for just me

A significant idea woman intended for me
Ideally, a woman I can say is ready for me
God's goal to open up my eyes to see this idea
woman
The greatest creation of my idea woman
Ideally, a woman that was created through God's
eyes for just me

Ideally, I am this woman's king as she places on
my head this crown
Being at my side with her hand in mines during
my hardest times of feeling down
Changing my face to new smiles removing those
old frowns
Putting me in my place when I am wrong just
before I start to clown
Ideally, a woman that is my ying as I am her
yang made for me
Idea woman for me that will never be the same
Ideally, a woman since birth made for just me
Ideally, a queen fit for this king

Kaiserrific

The perfect woman from my idea understanding
An idea woman who she is for just me…

I Wish Her To Be...

If I was given a chance to create my idea woman,
this is what I wish her to be…

I wish her to be a woman made from God
I wish her to be created with the beautiful
purities made from heaven
I wish her to be sweet
I wish her to be faithful
I wish her to be understanding and able
I wish her to be warm and soft
I wish her to be my one and every thought

I wish her to be a leader so that we can lead
together
I wish her to be my lifelong partner
I wish her to be someone that can go very far
I wish her to be unattached to any drama
I wish her not to cause any sorrow
I wish her to be a part of my tomorrow
I wish her to be my wife instead of being just a
baby mama

I wish her to be beautiful in her own skin
I wish her to be one with herself over and over
again
I wish her to be the one that uplifts her man
I wish her to be the one that teaches young ladies
to appreciate their men

Kaiserrific

I wish her to be someone that I can call my best
friend
I wish her to be someone that I can love with no
end

I wish her to be confident as Phylicia Rashād
I wish her to be as supportive as Coretta Scott
King was to Martin
I wish her to be as strong as Michelle Obama
standing besides Barack
I wish her to be as talented as Josephine Baker
I wish her to be as deeply cultured like Ruby Dee
and I am her Ossie Davis
I wish her to be as proud as I name some of these
proud women

I wish her to be as loving as my mother
I wish her to be a mother raising her children
right like no other
I wish her to be open with me never having to be
undercover
I wish her to be my one and true lover
As I wish to be her one faithful, loyal lover
I wish her to be a woman like no other from
before
I wish her to be…my dream come true…

Kaiserrific

As I notice in recent years some of our women have lost their place in society as to who they truly are. With the way that the media such as movies, music, and music video portray women, I felt that it was needed to write something to uplift. As society leaves mixed emotions, some of our women feel insecure about themselves because they do not belong with that "society". I wrote this to remind all these beautiful prodigies of who they are and what their worth is.

Beautiful Women: Powerful Words To Remember

Ladies when you feel unconfident about yourself,
look in the mirror and say these words:

I am a woman
I'm every woman
A beautiful woman
Courageous woman
Dedicated woman
Determined woman
I am the diamond of my world
I am in love with myself
I am comfortable being in my own skin
I don't need anyone to define me and my love
'Cause I love myself and that's all that matters
I hold the key to my heart,
For I am the joy to my world
I will always be the woman I am,
Whether I am young or old
I am a beautiful woman
That is real gold

Black Women, Love Who You Are...

Ladies, love who you are…
Love the beauty in your skin,
Love the woman within
We're not looking for you to be a Beyoncé or
Nicki to get our attention
Doesn't have to be America's Next Top Model
Remain proud and strong as it was created in
your profile
Continue being that beautiful prodigy that we
admire,
That beautiful queen God created that we desire

Love your melanin skin tone
Appreciate the complexion that spreads
throughout your body from the time you were
born
It's not the foundation or powder make up that
defines who you are
Never allow those chemicals to create the woman
you are
Your natural beauty makes up who you
are…your identity as I said
And as for those who are not sure, don't bleach it
just to fit in
Taking away from your personal identity will
never make you the same
Love the color of your skin and smile with it

Love your hair whether if its perm or flat ironed

Kaiserrific

We men will still love you ladies for who you
are,
As we love your long or short curls, kinks, twists,
and locks
Because we love every nap that you rock
And if you rock a great attitude with that style we
will never ask you to stop

Love yourselves whether you are big beautiful
and luscious,
Love yourselves even if you are small, petite and
thickalicious
Remember it's about what you like about
yourself a lot
Ladies remember it's your love that will make
our world rock
Holding a special place in our hearts, right here
on x marks the spot

Ladies, be proud of who you are within
Love yourselves first before you let someone put
their claim in
Don't let another person define who you are
Because your legacy as a black woman has come
very far
Be proud of this lifelong legacy of beautiful
black women
Women who paved a way for you to find your
inner goddess
You are worth more and never less
You are the queen of this castle

Kaiserrific

So don't waste it...
Remember, you don't have to be no Beyoncé or
Nicki to get our attention
No need to be a model or video vixen
Remain being that beautiful prodigy that you are
Ladies, love yourselves for who you are
Being the strong beautiful black women as God
created

A Good Woman

A good woman is like a highly paid job,
Only so few and so many get hired for the
position
Gets all the benefits
And gets to go home with a paycheck

A good woman is like my favorite car,
On a few can afford the tag price
And drive it off the lot
Having the privilege to drive it for so many miles
And can trade it for a better one

A good woman is like my favorite song,
Sings about it for a short time
Until the next hit comes along
Or until it becomes one your signature songs

A good woman could be like my favorite subject,
Study her for so long
Take the test to get it right
She is a piece of knowledge that I would have for
the rest of my life

A good woman is like my favorite sweet,
Tastes so good, such a true treat

Kaiserrific

She can give me diabetes
And I wouldn't care because she would be my
treat

A good woman is sign of hope
Makes the past pain go away
Reminds me of who I am
As she prays for me to be a good man

"Women in particular need to keep an eye on their physical and mental health, because if we're scurrying to and from appointments and errands, we don't have a lot of time to take care of ourselves. We need to do a better job of putting ourselves higher on our own 'to do' list." - *Michelle Obama*

We Are Women

(Lady Inspiration)

If a man doesn't wanna be your guy, don't trip
'cause he'll be beggin' to get with you later…
If that chick down the hall is gossiping about
you, she's just mad because she ain't you…
If you feel alone in this world, don't worry
there's someone else that feels the same way
So search for me and let's be friends
Listen to yourself,
Listen within your inner you; do you know what
she sounds like?
You sound downright pitiful because you choose
to deal with what this man has put you through…
You're so much better than that; don't take that
BS from anyone

If you feel men find you unattractive because you
gained a few pounds,
Don't sit there and being down about it,
Be about it and make a change…
You have control of your body that is your
temple
And that's what's precious about that…
Remember to love yourself first,

Kaiserrific

Because you are beautiful from the start if not
realized
But if you want to upgrade your looks, do it
If your one of those that feels the power of love
sits between your legs,
You seriously need a reality check…
Love is about your surroundings and how you
breathe love so spread it to other people…
There are people out there that are willing to
offer love that's not trying to get between your
legs…

You are women, the creation of the world since
the beginning of time
You are the strength of our children
You are the motivation of our leaders
You are the voices that wakes the world up
Preach the very things to us that our ancestors
preached to you yet we refuse to hear and or
listen…
You are the ones that inform us with vital
information needed to be heard…

You don't need a man to make you a woman
you're already complete
You don't always need the touch of a man to feel
good, touch yourself

Kaiserrific

You don't need someone telling how good you
look,
Look in the mirror your beauty is evident
You don't need a man to buy you things and or to
spoil you,
Go out and treat yourself and have a good time
Don't sit around waiting on opportunity to come
knocking on your door,
Knock the damn door down yourself
Make it your business to make the opportunity
happen
Turn the whole world around to make it
comfortable for you

Live your life according to your standards and
the right man will fall in place
Never allow yourself to be disrespected
Who wants to be called a bitch or whore?
If he's said it you then most likely he has said to
many women
That's the kind of disrespect you don't need
Don't allow any man to place his hands on you
every time he gets angry
There's no need for your eyes to be black
because he's mad at his homeboy

Just when you think life is perfect,

Kaiserrific

Bam!!!
He's the cause of your death,
Now there people crying over you at an closed
casket funeral
Because nobody wants to see a battered face
Wondering why you never cried out
Wondering where did they went wrong
Wondering if they ever saw the tell-tell signs
STOP!
RETHINK IT!
REVERSE THE CYCLE BEFORE IT'S TOO
LATE!!!

You all are women, beautiful women in fact!
You are the ones that make the world go around
You are the elements that make up the world for
what it is…BEAUTIFUL
You all are me and I am you
I love you dear women
Thank you for the uplifting days
The lonely nights talking on the phone
Thank you for your courage and wisdom
Thank you for taking care of our children
Providing a way for our homefront
Thank you for standing up in what you believed
in
Women thank you for being you….

What I Love About You...

Reason Number Two

"Women are the real architects of society." - *Cher*

My Future

I feel the chills passing through my veins each
time someone speaks of her name
I have smiles from here to space when I pass by
seeing her face
Silent moans leaking out of my mouth the
moment I touch her skin
Hard to hide what I feel when people notice my
thing for her when I start grinning

She's a woman not made for every man
She is exactly what I have been praying for
A woman that I have been searching for
She is everything I desire right down to the core
A beautiful woman with an unlimited look on life
She is someone more to me than just a man's
wife
With that said, she is my ultimate cure to eternal
life

Ok she got me feeling love struck
Maybe it's love or its pure luck
I'm caught up in giving her this exclusive
attention she deserves
I'm so caught up on her that I want to walk the
clouds with her into heaven
My treasure at the end of the rainbow as she is
the ultimate delight
One that I can't get off my mind throughout my
long days and weary nights

Kaiserrific

She is my outer surface that protects me
(*my protector*)
As her inner surface keeps me in suspense
Like every time she comes near me I'm stuck in
a trance
And when I smell her fragrance I just want to
follow her every command
Here I am addicted to this woman and has never
had a taste
Got me wondering what she'd taste like if I
placed my freeze pops on her sacred place
Probably tasting so good leaving me yearning for
a crave

For this is a woman I give her my very last and
share my all
Through my failures and success this is the very
woman that I would call
She is wonderful as she is great
The centerpiece to being my soulmate
For she is my woman
The woman
The only woman
My future…

How does a man find the right words to ask or say to a woman of his interest without it sounding like it's the same from every man? I wrote these series of questions in my poem "Can I" to have an idea of what men can say to deeply prove their interest in their women.

Can I

Can I have an intellectual talk with you?
Can I share a romantic moment with you?
Can I like you?
Can I fall in love with you?
Can I let what I been holding back come out to
you?
Can I express that I have a deep crush on you?
Can I make your wishes and my dreams come
true?

Can I come over and hold you real tight?
Can I lay with you every night?
Can I be with you for all the days of my life?
Can I be the one to call you my wife?
Can I be that husband you so desire?
Can I confess to you all my deepest feelings
because they feel so right?

Can I take you out on dates?
Can I make up for it now instead of beating
around the bush and waiting too late?
Can I get to know you for you?
Can I take your mind off of what you are going
through?
Can I do something really special to put a smile
on your face?
Can I do these things without having intentions
of wanting my flesh against yours?
Can I go walking with you through the park?

Kaiserrific

Can I sit with you to look at the moon and the
stars after dark?
Can I sit down and appreciate being in your
presence?
Can I continue to be a part of your world as you
are a part of mines?
Can I be the last face you see before you go to
bed at night?

Can I gain your trust?
Can I change your feelings to love instead of
engaging in lust?
Can I be myself with you?
Can I show you who I really am?
Can I allow the side me come out that you know
nothing about?
Can we go to a concert so that we can dance and
shout?

Can I be your best friend forever?
Can I be the one you share your secrets with?
Can I read poetry late night on the telephone?
Can I open my heart to you?
Can I grow old with you?
Can I love you forever?

Can I be everything that your last man wasn't???

Did I Ever Get To Tell You...?

Did I ever get to tell you?
That I wanted to explore a much softer yet
sweeter side of you, your heart
Lay side by side in our bed with you, locking
together never pulling apart
Having a million and one reasons to smile at you
Cherish every moment in this life with you
As I fall madly in love with you,
To grow as one whole completion with you

Did I ever get to tell you?
That I cannot keep my eyes off of you
Or how I want to share my secrets about things
that you never knew
According to how my feelings for you have
always been there
Holding back in my mind as I tried not to show
how much I cared
Being rejected by you was something that left me
scared

Did I ever get to tell you?
That I would think of many ways to say I love
you if I married you,

Kaiserrific

Count how many times as I call from work just
hear you say hello
Think of many times I've wanted to squeeze your
body if we were alone,
Not to forget how many times I lay in bed kissing
all over you just to taste your sweet skin
I want blush all day and night as I think of you
because you're worth my wild

Did I ever get to tell you?
That my soul channels into you,
We are spiritually connected as my psyche
belongs to you
It cannot take any big steps without you,
Or ever forget the songs that make me think of
you,
Holding future everlasting memories that I hear
of the tunes that reminds me of you
Like the first time we kissed would be so
incredible
These feelings shared between us are so
unforgettable

Did I ever get to tell you?
As I write these words on this page I dream of
your sweet kisses

Kaiserrific

Prays for you to be with me sharing those warm
blessings
If you haven't realized it but you are the woman
that I place in all of my wishes
And this feeling that is left over leaves me with a
smile throughout my day
Because if I ever had your love; it would make
my inner pains go away
Did I ever get to tell you?

I'm So Crazy About You...

I'm so crazy about you,
'Cause all I do is…think about you
Find myself writing all kinds of poems about you
Singing all sorts of love songs about you
I talk to all of my friends about you
I dream both day and night about you
Cause I'm so crazy about you

I see images of you in my sleep
You're on my mind is all I eat, think and breathe
Leaving your picture inside of my textbook,
'Cause your image is way better than reading the
words found in this book
Plastering posters of you all over my walls in my
room,
So I can see you as I wake up in my mornings
and before I go to sleep at night
Cause I'm so crazy about you

I can't wait to get to school just to look at you
Because your beauty in my view is way cool
Not knowing how to approach you makes me
feel like a fool
While the boys in class only want to screw, I
think so much more of you
Because I'm so crazy about you

I can't get enough of you; I feel a need for you

Kaiserrific

Everytime I eat, sleep, breathe is all about you
'Cause I'm so crazy about you
In my mind I just can't stop loving you
When I know really that it could be more of an
infatuation with you
Because I'm so crazy about you
You may think that you're the ordinary girl
But to me you are the girl
The one girl that I would love to give you my
world
Because you leave my feelings all in wind whirls
Each time you pass by playing with your curls
'Cause I'm so crazy about you

Yes I'm so crazy about you
It's something about you that leaves me feeling
good
Probably because you're not the average girl
from the hood
You are the girl that holds a big space in my
heart
'Cause I'm so crazy about you

Kiss of an Angel

Deep in my sleep, far away in my dreams
Where this beautiful woman appears placing
kisses
Caresses her hand to my right cheek
Sharing a connection between my face and her
soft chocolate skin

A distinguished beauty came from this woman
with this long black hair
Her body that was fit for a queen, telling me that
she was my queen
Got me caught up on her pretty brown eyes
She stands there in this striking pose smiling at
me
Expressing her message and purpose to my life
And how black women are the main purpose to
the black man's lifeline

It came to me that she was a goddess of love
A force with fire
And with her sweet kiss to my heart rose me
I smiled back to show my significance of
appreciation
Showing her the utmost respect
Giving her my loyalty to this woman
And my new found respect for every woman

She takes me down a path

Kaiserrific

A path which led us to our new found destiny
Where a man and woman can be one unit
A bond, a connection
One being formed together as one whole
Where our love was one thing,
That never broke us apart

Touching My Heart

I got to get to where you are
I wanna be where you are
I want to be always near and never far
I got to be in your arms
And share this love as one
Because you are worth every inch of the travel
And being one with you is where we need to
start…

When I see you, I see us writing our names
across the skies at night
Creating a whole new world with a whole new
meaning to life
If I was with you, I would dream of an
unconditional love that can go very far
Because if I was in your presence, we can reach
beyond the moons and the stars
Something that I would never take advantage
of…

Everytime I see your face, my feelings I just
can't hide
Not enough words in the dictionary can describe
your beauty
Because you can't just be called cute

Kaiserrific

You're way beyond any definition of sexy
And it's funny that when I see your smile it
leaves me in quivers
For you is a beautiful creation from God

A classy lady that I always fantasize about
The kind of lady that I can't live without
I get weak when I think of you walking around in
the same city as me,
Walking with those luscious curves showing off
your thickness,
Thickness a man like me loves and sees the
greatness
And because of you that I am addicted never
getting enough

I fantasize about playing in your hair,
In all its variations the curls, kinks, naps, and
touching it everywhere
I fall madly in love when I looked into your eyes
Glancing at your sweet soft succulent lips,
Because I lay in bed thinking about you the
moment before I go to sleep,
Dreaming that I am kissing them as I hold onto
your hips

Kaiserrific

I can imagine being around you would give me
butterflies,
Possessing something that unfolds my love for
you deep inside
Dreaming again about us being the king and
queen of the universe,
Taking small and big steps as one whole side by
side

I Miss You

I miss you,
I miss you each and every day
I pray for the day that you return back to my life
You the only woman that can breathe air into my
soul
Because you keep me alive
And with you gone,
I am another dead soul wondering amongst this
earth.

I miss you baby,
I miss you more than ever
I still remember back to those nights
The nights that we laughed,
We cried,
We loved,
And those special nights where we made love
Yes, the best love making I ever encountered in
between our sheets
The time that I spent with you were beyond a joy
to my heart.

I miss you,
I miss the woman that I have gotten to know and
love
The woman that can light up a room
The woman that makes my heart beat extra
harder,

Only because I was so nervous being around you
But you are the only woman that I prefer to share
all my love with
Truthfully speaking since your heart is attached
to mines,
So that makes us connected as one love,
That's what you call a special kind of love,
Only a few dream that their relationship can
become.

I miss you,
I miss you just because I do
I can't live another day in this life without you
I can't get you off my mind
When will you return to me?
Break the spell that is keeping us apart!
When will you end my sorrow with a happy
ending?
I ask for this wish because I truly miss you
I miss the only woman that truly loves me
Baby, I miss you…

Kaiserrific

What I Love About You...

Reason Number Three

As the author of this book, I want to express to every woman that has dealt with rape, if your voice hasn't been heard before, it's heard now. I may not know every woman exactly by name but you are not alone. I hear you and know of your struggle during with this difficult moment in your life. This is my chance to reach out to let each one of you know that it's someone that is concerned and cares. Please don't put this off and allow it to pass. Reach out and talk to someone to receive the proper help. I dedicated this poem to all the rape survivors because this is a very serious matter and was needed to be addressed. I along with other dedicated people will continue to reach out to any women that are victimized from rape. I love you all. Your voices will not be left unheard...

No One...

Will Understand Her Pain

As she silently cries out for help,
Feeling a coldness throughout her body as she
lay alone inside her bedroom
Developing sick twisted feelings going back and
forth through her mind
Blaming herself for what happened as her
innocence was taken away
And no one will understand her pain

Remembering back to that night when she asked
him to stop
Forcing himself as he pulled her panties off,
He tunes her out after he says no
Continuing to thrust inside her as she screams
begging him to stop
And no one will understand her pain

Fighting to save her life,
Trying break out of the tight hold he had over her
body,
He strikes her twice as he tells her that she feels
real good and nice

Leaving a permanent stain that she has to live
with for the rest of her life
And no one will understand her pain

Now a victim of rape
A new attachment to her life that she cannot
escape
Sitting up in the hospital for hours
Taking numerous amounts of test
A rape kit,
An HIV/AIDS test
Didn't make her situation feel the best
It much added on stress
And no one will understand her pain

She was so hurt as she felt so much shame
And as a rape victim people pointing at her,
Placing judgment on her while her rapist is
playing the blame game
Walking around as if he didn't do anything
Alone in the hospital taking the blame feeling the
shame
And no one will understand her pain

Walking with insecurity all around her like a cold
rush,

Kaiserrific

She is disgusted with herself with a development
of no trust
Feeling like her life is gone
Placing herself inside of this bubble of a zone
'Cause in her mind she feels cold and alone
Seeing herself as an embarrassment shutting
herself off from everyone
And no one will understand her pain

Although we cannot relate to your pain,
Or find the exact words to say
But you have our support through this hard
healing process
No one said that it was going to be easy
But we will comfort and listen as much as
needed

Because someone hears your cries
And it will be a shoulder to cry on
Someone knows that you are tired
And as you reach out to us for help,
We will help you start your life over
This is not the end for you
We are people that care and will help you
through

You are no longer the victim

Kaiserrific

You are now the survivor
We will shower you with lots of love as we
provide support
As we continue to believe in you
Allowing you to have time to heal for yourself
In hopes that in due time share your story with
the world,
To reach out and teach other women like you
About your pain and struggle as you cope with
being raped
And you too will save a life

As the subject continues to happen
And the world becomes even colder
Know that you all are never alone
And we will try our best to understand your pain

Survivor

Caught by her presence from the corner of my
eyes appears this beautiful woman
Beautifully defined through so many volumes
A nurturing woman that walked with her head
high no holding shame
A significant survivor of a double Mastectomy,
A procedure for breast cancer patients that
removes both of her breast
Comfortable in her own skin,
A proud woman that doesn't point fingers or
blamed anyone for what has happened
She accepts what God needed her to be

She opened up as she reached out to me and
spoke,
Trying to make it easy for me to understand by
making jokes
Shared her story of a trial and challenging
journey,
Easily expressed that breast cancer was her
enemy
As she faced a cruel reality of feeling less of a
woman
Left her feeling like she was fading, becoming
nobody

Kaiserrific

And how it destroyed not one but both her breast
Left her inner thoughts with a mental lapse of
feeling unloved
Insanely rejected by the man that said he would
never leave her side
But as he rejected her to being in his arms
It was a love that was once there but now is gone
Told her that she was not the woman he once
loved
All because she did not look like every other
woman
A woman that was thick, curvy with hips breast
and all

As I reminded her that she was somebody
Reminded her that she has an important place in
this unbalanced society
Taking her by the hand as I stood by her through
this journey
And I told her not to be afraid of expressing her
purpose
And to be never afraid of whom she was

But as her tears started streaming down her face,
A flashback to that nonexistent relationship
started happening

But remembered that she has to continue on
living,
And began loving herself first again
Searching for herself through a sacrificing path
In the end realizing that she didn't need breast to
make her complete

She knows that she is beautiful,
Absolutely complete,
A real woman simply a treat
One with a purpose as she shares her to tell,
Because it is other women that are too living
through this spell
Because she is my sexy as I appreciate the
company of this lady

Surviving through a life changing experience as
you acknowledge your value and your worth is
…WHAT I LOVE ABOUT YOU…

What I Love About You...

Reason Number Four

She Told Me Her Name Was Billie Jean

She told me her name was Billie Jean
A deep force struck our chemistry as we both
crossed each other in a scene
She explained how I was her day as I claimed her
as my night
These unexplained feelings captured between us
felt so right

She wrote the last sentence to her happy ending
with my soul
Making love to my exact words as she placed it
on paper
Using words so beautifully making it sound like
it was written in gold
As we got to know each other we built a special
relationship,
A deep connection between us which never got
old
A beautiful love between two people that never
been bought or sold
She's one woman I cuddle with on those days
when it gets real cold

She captured my eyes when we first met 'cause
she was so incredible

Kaiserrific

Entering my life with such a lovely presence
surrounding me was so unbelievable
I just couldn't stop looking at her 'cause she was
so irresistible
As my lips kissing on her neck she'd taste so
edible
She's the type of woman I can be myself as I get
comfortable
Whenever I see this beauty all I want to do is
hold her
She's a keeper, a winner, a star in my eyes that
she's irreplaceable

In my fantasies we made love for 40 long days as
we sexed for 40 long nights
Explored our chemistry stricken bodies as our
erotic minds traveled through time
In the process she caressed my thoughts
As she used all of her feminine temptations on
me getting my feelings lost

My future with her appeared in and out of my
faded dreams
She smelled so good having me caught up
Caught up on a love that was satisfying to my
every need
Indeed I realized that this woman actually loved
me
Believed in me,
Remaining loyal to me as she was my daily dose
of ecstasy

Kaiserrific

This woman was more than dreams she was my
reality

I admit that was one night that I was driven by
her madness
As her love making took away my pain and
sadness
Placing a smile on my face being my daily
satisfaction
The connection between us is a much deeper
attraction
No words spoken between us but expressed
mainly with our actions

Again she told me her name was Billie Jean
Mentally touching my softest side getting the
best of me
Left me falling for her for 40 long days and 40
desiring nights
She does something to me when she moves her
hands slowly across my chest
I immediately melt when she's caressing her soft
skin up against mines feeling her flesh
And as our bodies lock in between the sheets is
our business as it tells the rest

And I admit Billie Jean was my lover…

This Woman...

This fascinating woman intrigues my soul
Touches my heart in places that's never been
touched
Says things that I hardly hear most women
nowadays say
She is definitely a great reason for me to stay

To me she is defined as a true woman
Never had to be anything more but who she truly
was
A real woman placed into my world with a
purpose and cause
Not one that I have to always argue, fuss and
cuss
Touching me in more ways than one with love
than physically with lust

Whether she knows it or not,
She captures a place in my heart
A special place that any of my past loves knew
about
When I think of this woman my feelings rises up
to the temperature of hot
And in my world I place her on the top

Kaiserrific

Her love and worth is much more valuable than a
piece gold
She is one that I embrace myself with together in
a hold
Becoming a sculpture with this beauty in a
sculpted mold
Sharing the rest of my life with her even when
we grow old

Saying goodbye to her would be the hardest
things to live with
Because I prefer always saying to her hello
Like I can always tell her goodnight
When I know I rather say good morning when
she awakes

For now I patiently awaits when I am genuinely
hers
Waiting for this special day to unite with me as
one
Opening up new chapters to our life,
While putting our past ones come to a close
But I'm satisfied for now with us just getting our
start…

She

She is my comfort when I feel uncomfortable
She prays for me during my lowest time of need
She sees a royal substance and blessings inside of
me
She loves the man that's become of me
She loves that I am my own individual and not
being another

She can use her spirit to turn my frowns into
smiles
She has a gentle soul that removes the cracks
from my shallow
She's my Dr. Feelgood to cure me when I'm
lovesick
She always shows me respect
She is my opportunity when others didn't give
me a chance
She is what I been searching for deep within in
my soul
She is a woman that I love, cherish, and connect
together as a whole

She's been there for me through my late nights
She gets upset about her being M.I.A. from my
site

Kaiserrific

She appreciates me before she knew of my
artistry
She is the pen to my paper
She is like no other
She is not one that I hide or roll out with
undercover

She is my angel from the heavens
She was born to be made just for me
She's no Nikki, Beyonce, or Billie Jean
She doesn't have to be no Lil' Kim or a Queen B
She was created just to be my one and only

She gives me no reason to lay down with another
woman
She gives me no reason to feel like she has to
leave me for another lover
She's my motivation, inspiration and dedication
She is my determination for a better life
She's not girlfriend material but created to be my
wife

She…

My Moment With Black Love

I haven't known you for a long time but yet you
came into my life like a breath of fresh air
Mesmerized me from one ear to the other
Turning me on as you freely express yourself
The vibe connected between us was exactly
enough
Never forgetting how I confessed to wanting you
all to myself

Hearing the words come out of your mouth was
such a soothing force
Allowing me to tap into your inner goddess
You know the one that other men doesn't allow
you to release
You expressed to me with a warm felt tempting
ease
You didn't play any games nor were you a tease
You kept my attention on a lockdown and I was
pleased

Funny how time flies when you and I have fun,
Openly expressing our feelings about any and
everything
Diggin' deep within our souls

Kaiserrific

Saying what has been trapped inside for so long
One of the reasons why our spirits get along

When chemistry hit between us,
It ran so smoothly like a stream of water
As our bodies clinched passionately together
Being the right timing for you and me to engage
into each other
This special connection, this bondage between us
felt like no other
As black love was indulged it busted out like fire
and desire

In the aftermath I will always appreciate you,
I adore you
I admire you
Share a great love for you
This precious moment shared between us is one,
That will be remembered forever as I breathe air
out my mouth as I lay in my bed each and every
night
You touched my soul on so many levels before
the physical
Fed my brain knowledge as you made love to it
Nourished my emotions refreshing me that true
love still exist

Kaiserrific

And lastly locking my body with yours leaving
me speechless

*Damn...I love my moment with black love
especially when it's with you...*

Someone Who Loves You

I thank God for you each and everyday
You are the part of my life that keeps me smiling
I am so deeply in love with you that I find myself
crying
I know where my happiness went
As I share this time with you is well spent
And now I found it, I don't want it to ever leave
me
Just know this is the new beginning for you and
me

I keep going through your pictures just to look at
you
Looking at the images of you leaves me clueless
Keep playing back in my head how your voice
sounds to me
Thinking about how you touched me
The way I touched you
The way we shared love on several occasions

Yes I am someone who loves you
Yes I do need you
Yes I wake up desiring you

Yes I want you more and more that I think about
it,
I can't walk away from you
Walk away from us
Can't never turn my back on the history we have
together
I keep returning to this fascinating history as it
plays in the back of my head

I have always been someone who loves you,
Thought I would never found my match
Rocking this life together as one
As how God created the heavens and the stars
God created you in my dreams from beyond
Let's take that chance
Stand on that stance
Giving love its chance
When it's all over, I hope you say yes…

Kaiserrific

Spend the Night

Spend the night with me,
Let's share each other's time instead of some
physical intimacy
Lay under me as I hold you with my arms
Allow me to pamper you with my charms
Make this one night special
It's up to you, just answer my call

Spend the night with me,
Share the night with me
So that we can laugh or talk
Enjoy the moment as it passes by
Where you can be my girl and I am your guy

Spend the night with me,
As the Quiet Storm plays on the radio
A peaceful moment where the breeze is coming
through the window
Where our souls are pleasing each other beyond
ecstasy
This night with you is my life time dream

Spend the night with me,

Kaiserrific

As I kiss every single part of your sweet
chocolate skin
Lay back and enjoy every moment of this
innocent foreplay taking it all in
Where our skin touch as our bodies unite as one
Investing a well spent together
Sharing these precious moments with you and no
other

Spend the night with me,
Remember this moment in time of you being
with me
Engaging in something deep, soft, sensual
beyond intimacy
Place your heart against mines
Make this memorable for the both of us
So that way our souls together will be fed

Spend the night…

You Don't Know Me & I Don't Know You

(*The What I Love About You Version*)

Excuse me,
May I have a minute of your time?
This won't take too long,
See you don't know me and I don't know you
Well for starters my name is Chris but most
people know me as Kaiserrific
And your name is…???
That's a nice name,
You don't mind if I express my thoughts for
these last few minutes?

Now I never have done this before but..,
When I first seen you I wanted to talk to you,
Saying something really nice instead starting off
with something lame,
At the same time ask to take you out to a nice
dinner and movie
Share an interesting conversation and later share
a dance to our favorite song
As we out on the floor we can gaze into each
other eyes
Engaging in a passionate kiss

Kaiserrific

Embracing one another as we share this special
dance
Moving to the beat as it flows through our bodies
allowing time to pass

When our eyes first made contact, I wanted to
know exactly who you are
Started having visuals of us hanging out as we
share real fun times together
Leaving you with a good lasting impression is
what my heart wants
So that I can ask you out for another date and
after with no doubts,

The minute you entered in, I imagined showering
you with plenty of gifts
Either in person by me ringing your doorbell or
by special delivery
Letting me inside your secured heart and show
you a correct way to love someone
Allowing me to take my time in showing you
that I am the right one

Because baby the moment I'd seen you, I knew I
wanted to share my life with you
Share my last name with you,

Kaiserrific

Making this thing between us official being the
real deal
Ease you away from all the past pain; with me
being your new reason to heal
I want to love you so much that we continue this
into a next year and years after
I get weak everytime someone speaks of you,
You appear in every one of my dreams
But I know we're strangers
Two totally different people living totally
different lives
Never seen each other anywhere before
And you may already have someone in your life
If you did, how come he is not here with you on
your left side?
But I must confess, baby I am falling for you
The last thing I can remember left fresh on my
brain was you kissing my lips…
Reminding me know how soft yours were

But the minute I saw you, I wanted to hold you,
Providing you with every reason that my love
will always be pleasing to you,
An instant reminder that you can love again,
This connection between us so soon doesn't have
to end

Kaiserrific

So if this is not what you want from meeting me,
I have no problem being your friend
But I won't forget how I would leave kisses on
your neck as you giggle saying "Boy stop..."

But with you not knowing me,
And me not knowing you
Would you prefer that we travel around the world
viewing beautiful scenery from the mountains?
Ride with me across the country until the gas
runs out and the tires go flat
Spending a day at a carnival hand in hand
wearing those his and hers hats
Later stopping by our favorite restaurant filling
up on dinner as it hits the spot
Or how about a day of me pampering you
massaging all of your sore spots
I share my heart with you, as you unlock it with
your key,
These sentimental things are what my visions see

And the second that I seen you walk through the
door,
I wanted to give all my love to you
Sharing a memorable night of love and intimacy
developing a soft sensual chemistry
And the rest of what we do is history…

Kaiserrific

These are the things that ran through my mind
the moment I saw you
I hope that what I shared with you didn't offend
you,
But if you was my woman this is what I would
want for us
But again you don't know me and I don't know
you…

What I Love About You...

Reason Number Five

"I feel like every woman is a queen, and we should be treated as such, and we should, you know, sort of request that sort of treatment from others." - Queen Latifah

This incredible woman was placed on this earth to serve as the example of what a mother is supposed to be. I was one of the lucky ones to have her in my life. My mother goes out her way to help her children, her grandchildren and even her great-grandchildren if she could. To know that she walks the face of the earth with God in her life with such a warm heart, her elegance and grace is simply amazing. You can always replace a boyfriend, a girlfriend, a husband or a wife and find another. But you can never replace a momma. The way I feel about mines, she is truly irreplaceable. This is what I felt about my momma.

Kaiserrific

A God Given Queen
(*My mother, Roslind Kaiser*)

Momma always been at my side,
Through every one of my trials that I'd faced
Never turned her back on me, as if she knew it
was her place
As her child, I will NEVER turn my back on her,
To help her child like as a true momma would do
Always teaching me how to live right
But will get in my … when I was wrong
And I came correct when it came to momma

Momma took away from her own life to share
hers with mines
When she could of have been selfish with her
own wants, needs, and desires
But devoted her life to make sure that I had
mines
Always gone out her way to make sure that her
babies had the best
Being the best momma made sure that we'd
become
As she dreamed for us to be geniuses instead of
failures,
That's one thing I will never be in my momma's
eyes … a failure

Kaiserrific

I wondered if momma ever had dreams
And if so, what kind of dreams did she have?
Were her dreams of becoming something beyond
life?
Something beyond what any mom does in their
everyday life
I wonder if she still dreams about them as I do
And if she does, how can we make them come
true?
If not, I will see to it that my dreams are lived out
for hers

Wonder if my dreams were like my momma's
dreams
Did she ever want to be a singer, a writer, a
teacher, or even a doctor?
Maybe so because she had the gift to help a child
in need
Either by educating them, listening to them, or
even expressing her love to them
Did she dream of being a momma?
Or did she want to be the world's greatest
person?
No need to question that, because she's always
great to me

Kaiserrific

Always the perfect angel in my eyes when I think
of momma!
I wondered if I was everything that momma was
proud of
I wonder if momma felt she did everything to
make us proud
But momma didn't have to do much to make me
proud
I was proud from the first day I realized who she
was
Realized she was a woman that never abandoned
me
But when the time comes that she has to go,
She made it clear to remain strong
It will be very hard to let her go
She's everything and so much more to me
But that will be the time I have to go on with life,
My time as a man to live and grow

Like I said she has been everything to me
My educator
(*I wouldn't be able to read or write had it not
been for her*)
My role model
(*She did made sure we had manners and respect
towards all people*)
She is my hero

Kaiserrific

(*Always saved me when I was at my lowest*)
And I am her number one fan

I will never have another momma like her
Because it will never be another like her
And for that I will never take advantage of her
But I will take advantage of the time shared
To be in the presence of the woman that cared
I wouldn't be who I am had it not been for her
She plays a major part of my life
The one of who chose to keep me alive than to
take my life
Thank you momma,
And most importantly…I love you

Maya

She was our black queen
Our poetry queen
A phenomenal queen
And now this queen is in heaven reciting to our
king

She knew why the caged bird sings
Expressively wise with her words as she said
great things
Never afraid to telling the truth and shaming the
devil
As to why her work is left for many generations
to follow
She was one poet that knew her purpose
To her art and life on so many levels

Her family and close friends knew her as
Marguerite
But the world knew her as Maya
Either way, we love this woman
As she loved us
To inspire us
To motivate us
To uplift us
Most definitely to educate us

Not only was she a poet but an educator
Taught women that they too, can be phenomenal
And as she says Still I Rise gave us meaning of
new hope
Not only Maya was there with us through the
struggle,
But taught us how to deal with it as we cope

Maya Angelou was more than a woman
She was a matriarch of history
For us poets, our mother of poetry
She lived through the movement
She was a perfect example of true art
A woman of her own kind
Simply a beautiful woman with all heart that was
absolutely divine

Marguerite Ann Johnson aka Maya Angelou, we will always love and miss you. Thank you for the influence, the motivation, and most importantly the inspiration. Thank you for sharing your talents with us. As before, we love you and definitely miss you.

Kaiserrific

My Fair Belle

She's my hero
Always number one never a zero
A true woman to the uppermost
I'd say the word SUPPORT and she comes to
mind,
'Cause in my time of need she'd drop everything
to help me at no cost
I say the word FRIEND and immediately a great
connection comes first, never a loss
But together we share a beautiful partnership
that's best for business

This distinguished woman that walks in volumes
that I cannot describe
A legend long before her time,
A young woman with a flavorful old school soul
The descendant soul from great women from
another time of another place
As she speaks the words of the wise
She is absolutely the truth 'cause she will tell you
no lies
One woman I can say that recognizes one's true
gift as others denies

When I think of Belle Be,

Kaiserrific

Family woman comes to mind
A devotedly dedicated mother
A visionary like no other
A great friend,
A singer,
A creator of fine art,
Whose pure humbleness stole my heart
Listened when no one else listened
Understood when no one else understand
Absolutely believed in me so that I too can stand
Seen the best in me as she created the blueprint
to expand my talent

As for her haters she will be to them as cold as
ice,
Known to kill a person with kindness as she
remains nice
As her name Belle Be speaks to me in volumes
This beautiful masterpiece stops the world in its
tracks causing all problems
'Cause she is a new way of hope
For she is the future to new opportunity for
future artists in the world of art

*Thank you for showing me my worth and how I
can do so much more…*

She Is Not A Test

She is not a test!
I warn you that she is not a test!
She is her own revolution,
Not a detail or an illusion
Her words spit out like fire with mass fusion
Where the message and the definition of whom
she is creates the conclusion

Never a needy or mad sistah
Never the sad sistah
Always the glad sistah
But a friendly kind of sistah

She is not on that game targeting black or white
But the one that surfaces anything from the dark
into the light
And what she does to help our people is out of
sight
A woman serving the people during the day but
is a mother always by night
Go ahead sistah do your thang, it's dope fresh
tight!

Soul sistah number one!
As she takes the stage like it's her home
A beautiful queen in my eyes that holds the
crown
'Cause like James Brown, this sistah is super
bad!

Kaiserrific

Y'all know it when her message and delivery
goes in, she starts to clown

She is not a test!
She will preach and protest through hard days
and long nights
She's the sistah that will stand up for yo' rights
In the battlefield her spoken word is what wins
her day to day fights
Sistah we support you and love you always as
you put up the fight

A creative sense for she is that deal
Her purpose is to help those that needs to heal
Through her frustrations shows the madness
through her eyes
But only a few that know her,
Knows her request for love and harmony for
people is what she cries out

Be that I am a fan and a friend
A spiritual bond between two poetic powers we
will always have
For she is my sistah and together we share this
fight in the struggle
Spreading love and unity throughout the
community means more to her than some hustle

*Sistah Taraji, we love you and thank you for all
you have done…*

My Best Friend

You the one that I'd call when everything didn't
seem right
Always stood up for me when these chicks put
me down, putting up a fight
Opening my mind up to the new and fascinating
things in my life
I still remember how I would drive and you
always would be on my right
My best friend apart of my world, when other
females thought you was my girlfriend or wife

We shared the best of times
We shared the worst of times
But I have these memories to always remember
Because we were the best team players
Calm each other when we go through our anger
If you called me today and say that you needed
me,
I would stop everything that I am doing to be at
your service on one knee
Because you are my truest friend out of everyone
that came to me

As we share a love for the arts
And even though now we are far apart,

Kaiserrific

Our friendship holds a deep stain in my heart
One place not many traveled in my life by far
For being my best friend, I give you more than
five gold stars
Your babies are my nieces and nephews
As my son is your nephew
Like I feel my momma is your momma too
I can honestly call you my sister
As I would tell people that I am your brother
And our families are connected always
I always have a love and a respect for you and
your babies
My family always

Even though you are that cool brotha lady
But you are my best buddy
I will never forget you…
Because you seen the beauty in me
When everyone else thought of me as the ugly
You are my best friend and buddy
Even though we are far apart
And we can't hang out like we did from the start,
You always hold a special place in my heart
Because you was my friend from the very start
One that never put me down
But always uplifted me when I felt like my life
was falling apart

Kaiserrific

I will never forget our times out
Our laughs from silly jokes and conversations
Our travels all over town
Our late trips to Walmart and long phone calls
Our walks from your house to the parks
Our fun times going out to different restaurants
eat
Ending up at the Whole Foods trying all the new
and healthy treats

I love you my friend
My best friend to the very end
I miss every part of you
I miss our times together
Even though I still can call or email you
Not having you around at times, leaves me in
tears
You took away all of my pains and fears
But I understand you have your life
And I have mines
Because no matter what you are my best friend,
I love you

I dedicate this poem to my best friend forever,
Shayla. I love you…

Shea...
My Angel, My Sister

An angel is referred to as a person who performs
a mission or acts as if sent by God
If there was a woman that I would love to spend
the rest of my life with to learn, it would be her
I know that she has my back through the thick
and thin adventures of life
For that, she is forever a loyal friend from here
on out
I love and respect her, as if she was my deepest
and truest love
She's the main reason why I cannot separate our
friendship

When guidance was needed, she took me under
her wing and protected me
From everything that I need not fear in this life or
the next
She allowed me to not worry about what people
were going to say or do
She's encouraged me to be the very person I
needed to be...
Myself....

To know her, her beliefs, her life story and what she represents
Is the wisest decision that one has ever made
 She's a very special woman and not like any other woman I've ever met
Beautiful, intelligent, and a smart woman that's journeyed a road beyond words
Stories and experiences that come straight from her very own vision and life
But don't allow those beautiful long locks, that intriguing smile and gorgeous body fool you
She will stop you in your tracks before you can get the first word out
She's no joke on or off stage!

At birth, God instilled a mighty and raging fury into this woman
And with that wild force she's applied it to the pen and paper of her craft
Writing down things not of Greek literature but of real life and real people such as herself
When onstage she drives a force of fire all through her scriptures that comes out her mouth
Some wonder why she's so deep, strong, and is the real deal
But my overall opinion, her very name has a permanent mark on poetry

For many years she has captured the hearts of
many people including me
Touched the lives of people who has never heard
words like hers
A strong inspiration in me more ways than one
She is the force that other spoken word poets'
model after
To follow in my poetic sister's steps of success is
one that goes down in poetic history
Starts a new chapter of the successful creator
The next chapter of her legacy has influenced me
to write
For I am the struggling writer having a long way
to go,
From where she started with the first piece
I love you sis…
Thank you for everything!

*Dedicated to my beautiful and the most talented
poetic sister, Shea Brown....I love you with all
my heart and soul…*

My Friend, Dear Friend

My partner in crime from the very start,
My true friend indeed that will never part
She's my friend that holds a special place on my
heart
Regardless to what is going on with me you keep
me smiling
In dealing with her, she is a healing to my heart,

I am glad that she is my friend
Heaven sent at a point when I felt like my world
was at its end
The one that would give her last to put in my
hand
One friend that I can't stand to lose again

She works hard to have anything she wants in her
world
A real blessing of God's angels, I thank everyday
for knowing her
Known each other since my boyhood days
The very person I share my conversations,
Every one of my laughs,
As she's witnessed every last one of my cries
The very person would not fight but someone

that I trust my life

Influenced,
Inspired,
Motivated
Thank you God for this beautiful creation
I appreciate her through all our ups and downs
A man's true strength can be through his woman,
And she kept me strong when I felt down and weak
Believed in me from the first time we started to speak
I appreciate her for being my friend

Never my rival she's my influence,
Protected me through my times of worries pain
Wished we could have been around for all the years lost
But now at a great cost time has been made up
My good friend to help me to find light in my tunnel
I am so glad that she returned to my life, in my time of reunion,
Introduced me back to what I forgot was the meaning of life…

Victoria, thank you for this beautiful friendship…

Kaiserrific

"Who I be?..... I'm Lightning. .and my aura demands respect!!!!" - Poet Lightning aka Queen

Queen

The dictionary defines the word queen as the female ruler of an independent state, especially one who inherits the position by right of birth. The queen I know is like no other…

This queen is my reason why I love poetry
She makes me her message clear, for that she is
no mystery
The sistah is deep that I bow my head to her as a
member of her clergy
Listening to her words and some of her rhymes is
never enough for me
This is why I respect the aura of this beauty

This queen is as strong as a thousand powerful
black women united
Her words are fierce, being one of her greatest
weapons inside her universe
The influence of this woman bursts out like a
rock that hits my surface
As she is lightning striking through any storm as
her words move like the wind,
Because her movement is not something that
others can comprehend
This sistah that defines every letter of the word
friend
This queen is here always now to the very end

Kaiserrific

This queen was born a blessed beauty being my
modern day Cleopatra
Can walk in a room with bodacious hips and
nicely thick curves
Having all the heads turns as she strikes a pose
Delivers a message onstage that's always fresh
and never gets old
Because this queen is not your ordinary woman
but is doing extraordinary things

Men never open your mouth call this beautiful
queen boo or baby
Because that's not how real men properly
address this stunning lady
You'll never get a response 'cause she's not that
easy kind of lady
Like I said this woman's aura demands respect
And when this queen in return gives that same
respect back,
It'll leave you in a life loving, breath taking
effect

This queen is one of the mothers of our new
found spoken word legacy
Giving birth to a platform, a spotlight, a place
where us poets can be speak freely
Bringing out the best in us
Allowing us to define who we are,
She too defines excellence at its best
'Cause the beginning of her life tells us one thing
but her journey expresses the rest

Kaiserrific

One that I can say that this queen played a major
part of who I am
An inspiration to my heart, for she is my reason
that I write this piece

*Poet Lightning, thank you for being a very big
inspiration to me…*

Pam

I miss her smile,
As she enters lighting up the room
I miss her presence
I miss our deep talks
The kind of talks that can last for hours, weeks,
days, months a lifetime
Cause when I get mad ready to plot harm,
She'd stop me in my tracks being my alarm
I miss those times 'cause I was wrong and she
was right
I miss that firm believer even when stood her
ground putting up a fight
Not a day that goes by that I don't think about
her
She was a true gem through my eyes
A woman who was as close to me as an aunt was
to her nephew

I miss her sense of humor,
Having me crack up about some of the things
that went on at her day job
I miss how she kept me up on everything that
went on at our part time job
She was a real diva
One that could never be duplicated but often
imitated
Dressed in her own style as she represented
herself with class

Kaiserrific

Don't come at her the wrong 'cause that would
bring out her heat,
Be prepared 'cause they'll catch a fever
And when she's done cursing them out,
somebody would quiver
But once it's was over she would have people
respect her
Now she's with God listening to his word as he
delivers

Pam, I miss hearing your voice, seems like it's
been so long
Not a moment goes by without me bringing you
up
Because you witnessed a part of me becoming a
man as I grew up
Believing in me from the jump start
One of the reasons why you held a special place
to my heart
A place inside that will never separate or grow
apart

I never had the chance to say goodbye
Its hurts me that you left within the blink of an
eye
But it was time that God's called for you to come
home
And as much I want to but I can't be selfish
I must accept everything for what it is even
though it wasn't right

Kaiserrific

At least you don't have any reason to fight now
You are now free so that your spirit can be at
peace
So I will remember and enjoy my time with you
while you was here with me
I miss you dear friend
I didn't know that our time together would go so
fast to a sudden end
I can't wait till we meet again
So no goodbyes but see you later
I love you always my friend

Dedicated to Pamela Champion (1961-2012)
with love, I miss you…

If I Could Share, One More Night

If I could share one more night,
Would be the greatest feeling
'Cause she was too young to leave me
When we met she was only seventeen
I referred to her as my one and only queen
And she always called me her king
She said that we were meant to be
I thee wed my vow to be

We were deeply in love
As we both praised to God above
Thanking him for bringing us to together
Neither nor she or I would know that we would
be separated
That was the day that I dreaded
Because she was my strength removing my
weakness
This love for one another was my joy and my
happiness

She's now gone and I'm here
Back then we didn't live far as our love grew
close and near
Not a day goes now by that I don't think of my
sweet sweet dear

Kaiserrific

Playing our favorite song that we'd danced to
every year
Remembering those good times we use share
Remembering how much I would look into her
eyes as I would stare
Stare into the loveliness of the woman that was
my beautiful wife
I still love her even though cancer took her life
I still think about her every night
As she dealt with days, weeks, and months
putting up a long and hard fight
Standing up for what she felt was right
From here on out, I will think about my dream
girl for the rest of my life
Ain't I entitled to that right?

She will always be,
The one that meant so much to me
Always my baby, my queen
And I'll always be her king
If I could share one more night

*Dedicated to my friend LaShawn Glass and every
special woman we lost to any forms of cancer…*

Aja

A *true inspiration to all of us*
J *ustifies her ambitions as she goes on her*
mission
A *trooper to the art of poetry as she aids in*
helping all of mankind

She brings the best out of us,
Inspiring us to go beyond our limits
Allowing us to see opportunity where it is needed
Because she believes in us as we believe in her

My good friend as she is to all of us
Her inspiring words are so dope,
A unique style and vision expressed in her
messages are so tight
The one person that fills up many venues in one
night
She Is Poetry in her own right,
Finding her own personal power with her
adversities as she puts up a fight
Changing lives including mines through this
struggle helping us find our *refuge*

No stranger to the pen as she writes about life
across the skies

Kaiserrific

She performs for me
She performs for you
She performs to educate our children
She performs to educate our fathers
She performs to educate our mothers
As she brings black men together letting the
world know that we are not the enemy
As she is openly expressing that we are heroes
It's one of her visions to bring us all together
through God's harmony
My heroine as she performs and uses Hip-Hop to
deliver her message

Never selfish as she couldn't be defined as stingy
A woman that helps the homeless with the uses
of her art
She will give you the shirt off her back
Such an unconditional love for all of us that
comes from her heart
Like I said, she can bring people together
One of the reasons that we remain close to her,
never breaking apart

*I love you my friend Aja LaStarr, thank you for
all you have done. You are a part of me and I am
a part of you...*

My Wonder Woman

Born with ambitions that fulfilled all of her
dreams,
Carries her determination as it drives my
motivation button
A friend forever that most people don't have a
connection tied
One friend has never slipped up or came to me
with lies
A true friendship that will never be denied
Mea my truest friend to the end

She is one that appreciates another one's art
An artist herself in rare form
Proven many times that she can do anything
Starting her own business when the job market
knocked her down
Networking to create platforms for other
companies
Mastering in all sorts of technology shows her
passion into it
A deep determination of hers from the very start
Having no room for limitations to keep her from
fulfilling her dreams
She worked hard becoming a master at her own
thing

Kaiserrific

An extraordinaire career woman proven herself
to be
A loyal mother putting her babies first is what
they've gotten to see
'Cause people once thought that was something
that she couldn't be
But with patience and time she mastered being a
mom for she and he
Setting the bar displaying examples from her
own life,
Explaining the rules in dealing with society when
they're wrong or right
Setting life goals so that her babies future lives
can be easy
So they won't have to experience the troubles of
struggle she's dealt with

Not caught up on stereotypes of what women
can't do to discourage her
It made her more knowledgeable of these
situations
Through hard work, determination, and self
driven motivation made her an achiever

She's the perfect example of what a hard
working woman is
Living up to her dreams,

Kaiserrific

Promising not to allow the world to make her a
failure
I am proud to call her my friend
She's my wonder woman
To me she's a real hero

*Mea, thank you for being there through my
accomplishments and struggles, a true friend
indeed*

The Songstress

(Raye Cole)

It's hard not to admire a beauty that comes with
the beautiful sound her voice makes as she sings
A natural born talent that has always been her
thing
The way she can crowd a room says amazing
things
With the way she sings, music will never be the
same

I enjoy seeing my favorite singer onstage with
those dreamy eyes
She starts the first note; I can hear the sound
waves as it moves
The tone from her voice sends me into wild
grooves
But again I am just the guy that came to hear her
song
Never would I thought I would fall in love,
Falling in love with the fact this woman that
loves her art

Beautiful songstress I notice how you sing within
your soul
Because my feelings inside start getting out of
hand becoming uncontrollable
When I hear you sing, I feel like I'm the only one
you're singing to

Kaiserrific

What I hear from your mouth that goes through
my ears pulls me through many storms
Removing my cloudy skies as I'm floating on
this natural high

Before anyone knew of you, I had a little crush
on you
Before the recordings, before the performing I
caught onto the real you
Who would have thought or ever knew,
That because of your music that I would be
inspired by you
Falling for the songstress that lives in you
Admiring your distinguished style of music,
Beyond than what other men had on their mind
was…to do you

Beautiful songstress let me stop right here and
reveal the things that I love about you,
Like your beautiful long locs that fit with your
pretty milk chocolate skin
And as you step to the mic with those plump
juicy lips that mesmerizes me
Body perfectly shaped as it balances out with the
beautiful features of your face
Who cannot forget the lungs! Lawd those lungs!
Yes God gave you a pair of lungs because the
projection that comes out of your mouth is a
beast

Kaiserrific

I know with a sweet yet fierce sound like yours
someone can hear you all the way in the Middle
East
But the best man won your heart, so this part of
my chapter I must close…

But beautiful songstress remember that,
I am always proud of you
I will never forget the woman who sung a cover
song or two
That went on to sing her original tune
I'll never forget you,
I'll always play you in my ear
Whether it's during day or late at night,
Even if I warm or cold this beautiful sound you
produce never gets old
I will still hear the sweet sounds that comes from
you playing over and over in mind
A sound that never dies…

*On the stage, you share a special place that
touches hearts because you are The Songstress…*

Kaiserrific

"Women need real moments of solitude and self-reflection to balance out how much of ourselves we give away." - Barbara de Angelis

Woman Earth

Thinking about you makes me remember of
sweet summer mornings,
Where I'd smelled the fresh roses outside my
window
Enjoying the view of your beautiful morning
glow
Appreciating the beauty of your early morning as
the sun arises
While I hear the birds chirping as they sing your
favorite song in the trees
Along with the sounds of buzzing in the meadow
from the playing of baby bees

You make me appreciate my remaining time left
in this beautiful world
Being witness in your presence of daylight as I
am able to walk around,
Hearing your wind coming in my direction as it
picks up sound
Enjoying every moment of it brushing against
my face
Captivating this satisfaction during this moment
of nature inside this beautiful place
Feeling every bit of your warmth at the same
time taking your cold
Some of things in this past time that never gets
old

Kaiserrific

As I pass by the lakes and I see the trees
reflections off the glare
The sun shines even more radiant as your
reflection stands out there
The images of you are more to me than just a
stare
For me sharing my life with you is more than just
a care
I am one with you as you are one with the world

But you being a part of this earth God made this
into existence
You being one with Mother Nature
I can be assured that being with you that I have
no fears or dangers
Thank you for your love, contribution and
endeavors

Because you are the main part of the root that
started it all,
Allows me to appreciate you for more than your
worth
I love you Woman Earth

Pacia, thank you for your heart felt influence....

Work of Art

(Inspired by the art work of Michelle L. Artist)

I have eyes for you
Something that people never knew
The feelings has always been there
Haven't tried to make a big deal out of it or made
it aware
To be safe, I tried many times to keep it out of
my mind
Trying my best not to reveal how much I cared

OMG!
OMG!
You should have been with me,
Instead you chose him over me
Because you would never have to worry about
me trying to leave
You and I were definitely an item made, is what I
believe
You held the camera and all I ever wanted was to
be your work of art

I would do anything to be the picture you're
painting,
To have my face in front you,
Is like to love you,
Better yet to be in love with you,
You painting me, would be one with you

Kaiserrific

I never forgot about you,
I never forgot how we first met,
How you took an instant interest with my eyes
Imagining that you captured me as your first
masterpiece
I never forgot how beautiful you were
I never forgot how I thought you were the best
Everything that you did where my eyes can see it
was the best
From hearing the sweet sounds coming out your
voice to how you draw me on the canvas
And even now through all of your trials and
struggles I still think you are the best

I love you, for who you are
I love the woman you've grown into,
I love how you have mother wit in you
I love the personality of you,
I love how you can survive a struggle and not let
it keep you down
I love the artist in you, such unique styles
I love you and that won't ever change…
But baby what you are going through is just a
test,
Just a test
God will provide you with the rest
As I said before you will come out of this being
the best
And as always I love you
You hold the brush and I want to be your work of
art

Kaiserrific

Being a genuine collection of art that holds a spot
in my heart,
One of the reasons why God never let us to fall
apart
I need you more than you know
I need for us to be together and grow old
But I am like a canvas waiting for you to apply
the first colors on me

I know that I am not the man that you want,
Because that other one still holds a place to your
heart
But you capture a special place with mines
As your friend, I can't keep allowing you to go
through this man whirlwind of rhymes
And I know you love him but all I ever wanted
was to be your work of art
The center of your masterpiece
Through your art, you paint my emotions
As your photos touch of my heart
Thinking about how I wish I was your work of
art
The art you created with love
The colors you spreaded across my canvas with
your passion
Being the finishing product, a creation that was
captured through your eyes
An appreciation between the art and the artist
A special bond I want to share with you

I know that I cannot say exactly what I truly feel about you because of all the circumstances. But you mean so much to me and I would never stop feeling the way I feel. When I am in your presence its heaven on earth and I can only say thank you for being in my company. You know it's like the saying one man's trash is another man's treasure. In my eyes I never saw you as some piece of trash but a beautiful work of art. A work of art that needs to be acknowledged and displayed so that the world can appreciate it for the beauty that you hold...

Kaiserrific's Angels

These are not your ordinary women
They are angels heaven sent
Sent to always keep me smiling
Through their words in writing and spoken word
poetry
Something that's kept the hunger in my soul
satisfied
Through my eyes they're my treat and that's
tantalizing
I love every last one of them the same as my
feelings for them are equally divided

Can't get enough of these angels when they are
in their element
Each holds a special place of sentiment through
their art
Never phony or fake, these ladies speak solely
from their heart
I have so much love for each and every one of
them from the very start
My dearest friends for life that I will never
separate or fall apart
Angels sent to heal my heart

These ladies are dynamic
Their words are forreal
They are the real deal
Because of their hard work and determination,

Kaiserrific

Each one of these beautiful angels are
contributors to my motivation
I don't know what I would do if I didn't have any
of these special ladies as my inspiration
They are my reason to write this special
dedication

So through their vivid expressions of struggles
and strife,
Every last of one of these talent ladies see to it
that their voices were heard through the mic
Thank you my beautiful angels for dedicating a
little of your time to my life
Because without each one of you it wouldn't be
no Kaiserrific and that wouldn't be right

Dedicated to these beautiful angels:
Angel Davytaylor
Chantell McCline
Charisma Blue
Ell Bell Authorandpoet
EmCee
Fior Baptiste
Jai Elle
Jahlel Touche'FifthDegree Burns
Sensations of the Truth
Lilly Mac
Nicole Humphries
Poetic Slang
Ree Cee
Ronda Goolsby
SistaSols
*Tru_Starr_*
Yashi McGowan

"Beautiful Sistas,

The best thing you can do for you is love yourself. Let them love another. God has been waiting on you to be you for awhile now. So he can be the one to show you how you should be loved in the first place. Let the lesser love go, go for the greater and one day it will manifest as a man in front of you. When it is time and when you are ready." - X Blu Rayne a.k.a. Poetic Butterfly

Kaiserrific

Poetic Butterfly

I always seen you as an innocent caterpillar
blossoming into a poetic butterfly
Finally your chance to soar beyond the skies
Allowing God to help you find yourself as he
uses you for a purpose
Realizing that you are way beyond than the
content of your worth
With you knowing that, you were able to float
across the seas
Becoming one with your inner soul as nature
connects with earth,
Overcoming the surroundings of a harsh reality
Changing your past atmosphere, creating a new
one
Living with an unenthusiastic ambiance where
you'd overcame it all with triumphant victories
Removing all negative forces in your direction as
you continue to produce a much better you

Poetic Butterfly,
You've told us of your dreams as we seen you
lived them, encouraging me to live out mines
Throughout your life you dealt with inflicting
pains of the past to your present,

Kaiserrific

But as you evolved into the woman you've
become, you healed your wounds to preserve
your future
Living with the earliest of your precious
innocence snatched away from you
To having cloths of both betrayal and deceit
wrapped around you from those whom you
thought were closest to you
Normally this would have drawn a person to a
much darker side with no return
But you poetic butterfly,
Just when you thought you grew weak, your
struggle allowed you to grow stronger
Spreading your wings in a much higher spiritual
echelon
Never allowing the haters to break you
Not allowing these stereotypes out there to crush
you
Stopping anyone in their tracks before they try to
make a fool out of you
Yes my friend, you are unbreakable

But my Poetic Butterfly,
What man wouldn't desire such a woman of your
stature?
Admire the passion you believe in

Kaiserrific

Understand your creativity as flows through
many papers and pens
Obtaining a deep natural love that not many
poets know of
You are a fine example of what a woman is…

Poetic Butterfly,
You seek your salvation as you were sitting in
the snow
As you blossomed into this courageous woman
from holding Heaven's Key
My beautiful Poetic Butterfly,
Your verses in poetry are like songs to my
dreams
Your yearning to educate me and others through
poetry excites me
Because the intelligent mind you possess speaks
to my heart
The energy you bring to the mic uplifts me
Inspires me in ways to express freely through the
universe
You define me as to where I am proud to call you
sister as you call me your brother
A true divine, deep, and uplifting sista as you
bring it to the stage

Poetic Butterfly,

Kaiserrific

Your poetry will forever touch our hearts
Using those words that defines us all
My friend, you are one with the stars
Reaching up and beyond touching near and far
Never are you a fallen star
You're truly a deep sista speaking out with a
cause

*X Blu Rayne a.k.a. Poetic Butterfly, you are now
a shining star…*

What I Love About You...

Reason Number Six

"We are braver and wiser because they existed, those strong women and strong men... We are who we are because they were who they were. It's wise to know where you come from, who called your name." - Maya Angelou

Adam and Eve

(*Kaiserrific Style*)

I am her Adam and she is my Eve
Came together from the wonders of what God
created us to be
Sharing an open communication with one
another
Valuing our honesty as true love comes together
Understanding the definition of what it is to be
the other
And this is what makes our love different from
any other

As God's number one couple
We are together the mountains, the oceans and
seas
We are the surroundings of life that completes
great things
Removing our weakness because we are each
other strength
It is more to us than what's underneath the
clothes where flesh exists
We are Adam and Eve, a man and woman
created from God's seed

Eve is my goddess, my queen, my backbone
I give her the world
For I sit beside her as she sits on my throne
Because her final decision over everything gets

the job done
When it's all said and done, she is more likely
right when I could be wrong
'Cause my woman is the ruler of my kingdom

As I am her Adam
By God it's my purpose to be her protection
Providing her with love, trust, commitment and
attention
Walking side by side going together into God's
direction
As her king it's my duty to make sure she
remains my queen
Because the love I got for her is an incredible
thing
With us we are not about a power or control
thing
It's about compromising a plan to share our life
away
Not about the arguments of who is wrong or right
It's about what God has for us to determine the
rest of our lives

Remember no arguments, no fights
No going to bed not saying anything to each
other at the end of the night
No disagreements when we have time for
compromise
Satisfaction, determination, motivation along
with inspiration is what this couple share inside
God's true love is what we contain inside

Kaiserrific

Through it all and till the end
We are lovers and best friends
Here for one another to the very end
For she would get my last breath so that she can
live again
'Cause I am her Adam and she is my Eve
That's how it is as how God made us to be

"I'm not alone, I'm free. I no longer have to be a credit, I don't have to be a symbol to anybody; I don't have to be a first to anybody." - Lena Horne

Beyond The Beauty

It was said that beauty is in the eyes of the
beholder,
But when I see her beauty it's beyond the
woman,
Beyond the image that most men depict of how
she supposed to be as they attempt to lust after
She tells a story of significance as she poses with
her smooth skin and luscious curves
Reveals to all of us that her body is her temple
Her eyes tells about her pain
As her heart reveals her sorrow
While one sees the essence that shines through
her
For that she is true to her soul,
Knowing that her love is deep and shall not be
wasted
For she is fragile and must be handled with care
And if any man that encounters this beautiful
piece shall hold her love with a delicacy
As she overcomes her life storms remaining
strong, for she is a survivor
A sensual piece of art in the collection beyond
the physical appearance of what defines beauty

Dimes of Hip-Hop, Rap and R&B
PART I

Lauryn you created music as the sounds spoke to your heart
As how I wrote poetry deeply from my heart
Designed from a significant amounts of influence from art
The roots of R& B flow through getting your start
But Hip-Hop is where you made your birthmark

While I'm inside your world where *Everything Is Everything,*
You touched me on familiar sounds with new styles as she *Doo Wop (That Thing)*
Killing Me Softly to your songs as if *Nothing Even Matters*
Producing *The Sweetest Thing* of sounds I ever heard
All the way from dealing with the *Ex-Factor* to discovering *The Lost Ones*
But I *Can't Take My Eyes Off You* cause the music keeps me feeling so brand new
But *Tell Him* like you did *Zion* as to why *When It Hurts So Bad* referring to your miseducation

With him being *Mr. Intentional* I understand why you send yourself on another path

So as the beautiful Queen Latifah introduced her *Wrath of My Madness*
Made it clear that *Ladies First* and that's how queens treatments should be
In her time living *Just Another Day* she screamed out to both men and women about *U.N.I.TY.*
Speaking on issues about the disrespect of women in our society along with harassment and domestic violence

So through the music and movies she searched for her *Weekend Love* instead she *Set It Off* by *Living Single*,
Later kicking it at the *Beauty Shop* with her girls by *Bringing Down The House* for *The Bone Collector*,
Spreading some *Joyful Noise* at *The Cookout* in the *Secret Life Of Bees* in *Chicago* on *The Last Holiday*,
Being the *Perfect Holiday* for all of those lovers that want it *Just Wright*

Aaliyah *At Your Best* you had us going *Back And Forth* reminding me that *Age Ain't Nothing But A Number,*
You made me feel like that *One In A Million* as you asked me *Are You That Somebody?*
But *I Don't Wanna* brag but you were so irresistible that my focus remain in your direction
Sending me that *4 Page Letter* but *If My Girl Only Knew* it would have been *Hot Like Fire,*
'Cause you would have been *The One I Gave My Heart To* 'cause I too was a *Choosey Lover*

Through my sacrifice *The Queen Of The Damned* said *We Need A Resolution* as to how we *Rock The Boat*
And if we didn't succeed you said to dust yourself off and *Try Again*
But you were *More Than A Woman,*
When I went away to search for my destiny you asked me to *Come Back In One Piece*
But by the time of my return God called you home
And Aaliyah even though you are no longer here *I Care 4 U* always, I *Miss You*

Lisa "Left Eye" Lopes I know you was with yo' girls TLC when you *Ain't 2 Proud 2 Beg*

Putting yo' *Hat 2 Da Back* and broke it down,
On your lyrical influence to *What About Your Friends* defining the real from the fake
But it was brilliant how you *Creep* on me with *Waterfalls* explaining real life through music
So you *Baby, Baby, Baby* you had me *Diggin' On You* when we was vibin' in the *Red Light Special*
Left you with some *Girl Talk* to discuss about me 'cause you know it's *No Scrubs* over here

And always along with T-Boz and Chilli you made sure that we didn't feel *Unpretty*
But to remember you Lisa, you'll always be *Untouchable*
'Cause *A New Star Is Born* as you are creating new sounds in heaven
But we will never forget you my love, see you at *The Block Party*
A musical genius of *Supernova* creativity
I promise you will never be forgotten...

These are my genuine dimes of Hip-Hop, Rap, and R&B
Women who worked hard pursuing their dreams
Creating a musical history

Designed from a fine timeline of well polished legacies

To be continued...

Beautiful Bubble

I look beyond everything that people have seen
about you
Ignoring any negative comments made about you
In my eyes you were more to me than what men
thought of you as some wild sexual freak
Wanting a big part of your heart but first I must
get inside with a peak
Like knowing the real you
Instead of the assumptions that everyone else
made out of you

I don't love you just for your bubble butt,
My feelings for you are coming out deep from
my gut
I see a great woman inside of you,
When it comes to the real you, some men or
women would never know or even have a clue
Because to me you were more to me than just
some chick that I can lick,
Far from a woman that I want to just stick

I want to explore you,
Sit back and enjoy every moment that I have
with you
Share a little fun as we engage in a laugh or two

Kaiserrific

As we cuddle up on the couch with the privilege
for me to touch your skin
Enjoying the moment when began to explore me
too
Having the opportunity to being your man, I
would make sure never ends

Yes I have thoughts about you,
With you already knowing that I truly admire
you
Fantasizing every night about me making love to
you
As I said before, you are more to me than just a
screw
Yes I want to surround my world around you
Build up a different type of connection between
me and you
And if I chose the last woman on earth to walk
with me, I want her to be you

My beautiful bubble,
I want to spend the rest of my life with you if
that's no trouble
You don't know how much I desire you
I will climb mountains and swim seas just to get
to you

Kaiserrific

You can be in a crowd of a trillion people and I
can still see you
I can't go a day without thinking about you
Singing out your name,
Writing it out in my notebook as I trace it over
and over
Having make me feel so lucky, I swear you were
my four leaf clover
Closing my eyes at night imagining how it would
be to kiss your sweet lips
Caught up in my deepest fantasy with me behind
you with my hands on your hips,
Off the edge of my bed on your knees making
sure you don't slip
Feeling the passion shared between us as I feel
my manhood inside you taking a dip
Spreading my hands across your soft chocolate
skin
Living out all my wild and crazy sexual fantasies
of you is just the beginning

Truthfully you are my beautiful bubble,
Let me explain my feelings if that's no trouble
I have this deep thang for you
But I know that I can't have you
Imagining me being with you like is a fresh
breath of air

Kaiserrific

Only to know that I wake up you won't be there
But this daydream playing in the back of my
mind, you'll always there

I'll always think of you my beautiful bubble…

"Women have always been courageous... They are always fearless when protecting their children and in the last century they have been fearless in the fight for their rights." - Isabel Allende

Mothers

Thank you for being in our lives for all these
years
Checking to see if we need to be fed or our
diaper needs to be changed
Making sure we were taught to walk and talk
Constantly going over our ABC's and 123's
Teaching us how to write our name and to read
so we can understand words
Taking out time to explain what's right as you
showed us what is wrong
Teaching us how to treat people as how we want
to be treated so that we can get along

Thank you for waking us up for school
Keeping our clothes looking nice and clean when
you could have worried about yourself
Then later either walking or driving us making
sure we were on time for class
Thank you for introducing us to a new sound as
we listen to your music
Reminding us every day about our history in
hopes that we become better people
Sharing these precious moments as a family
creating our own history

Even though sometimes we didn't want you to be
right yet you were
Doing what you had to do because you cared and
loved your children

Kaiserrific

Sparing your last when we needed showing your
unconditional love
Using it to protect us as we dealt with real life
pain while experiencing true hurt

We know that you all can't always be there at our
aide everytime
And your time when you will have to leave us
So you all leave us with a thousand morals
To come up with 99 solutions instead of leaving
us with 99 problems
And if we need you, you'll be there within a
blink of an eye
Showing us truths instead of feeding us lies

Thank you for keeping us off the streets
Keeping the abuse, alcohol and drugs out of our
site
Teaching us to be responsible even when dad
wasn't around
You always had our backs when no one else was
around
Thank you for being the chosen one to be our
mother as you raised us
Making sure that we grew up to become good
people
Thank you for being our heart as you continue to
love us

Thank you moms for never abandoning us
(Being there everytime we come home)

Kaiserrific

Never giving up on us
(*Taking the time to show that you love us*)
Never removing us from your life
Never turning your back on us
Showing us that we were number one always in
your life
Being there through all of our struggles and
stressful fights
Dealing with our pain when no else could
understand
You will always be mother because you earned
and exercised that right

*Dedicated to every mother in the world, thank
you for loving us…we love you*

Secretly In Love With You

When I think of you,
I instantly want to talk to you
After seeing a picture of you,
Capture myself inside an image with you
Knowing that I can't have you,
I find myself desiring to have you
Be nice if I could love you forreal
Maybe I'm secretly in love with you

To know that I have this major crush,
Thinking about you gives me an adrenaline rush
I would do anything just to feel your touch,
Touch of your warm soft skin
Thoughts of loving you are growing within
Where I wanna share my life that allow to let you
in
Like holding you at night so we can see the moon
In hopes what I feel for happens soon

In reality you is all I want
I'd give the better half of my world,
Provide you with every piece of silver and gold
Live out an enjoyable life with you from young
to old
Be your warmth when you're feeling alone and
cold
But I know that's not enough
Because I wasn't him

Kaiserrific

Nor will I ever be
Whether you believe it or don't have a clue,
Woman I'm trying to tell you that I am secretly
in love with you!

My Big Beautiful Women

Absolutely the most beautiful and simply so
exquisite
Summing up my BBW loves with two important
words dedicated and determined,
My kind of women that definitely gets my
attention
Big and thick, beautiful all the way around, filled
with lots of love
Exclusively beautiful women created from the
man above
Make me feels good every time I get one of their
hugs
I enjoy the squeeze so much that I don't stop till I
get enough

To my plus size cuties
Truthfully speaking you all is most men's
fantasy,
The ones that dresses sexy showing off your
luscious curves
Making most men's head turn
Having every last one of us including me feeling
weak
I know when you all pass by me I can't stay in
my seat

My beautiful BBW women,
I love you, you, and especially you

Kaiserrific

I love every part of you
From the appearance of your curvaceous
thickness,
To y'all beautiful attitudes in this society with a
confident self esteem
I cannot walk through this world and not
acknowledge your presence
You all play a key role to life
As I see the greatness of you ladies seen through
my eyes
The sexiness that comes from y'all as it tells the
truth that shames the lies

My big beautiful women from me to you,
My attention can't resist you,
Can't get enough of you
My heart desires when it comes to every one of
you
I have a great desire for you plus size beauties
I appreciate every bit of your presence
Taking sexy beyond a whole new level
(*Letting it show that you don't have to be no size
4 but you too can be sexy in a size 24*)
You plus size loves are always needed in my life
You all are everything a husband needs for a
wife

To every beautiful BBW you all are a flavorful
taste of women greatly appreciated, thank you
*What I Love About You...IS THE BIG
BEAUTIFUL WOMAN IN YOU...*

"I believe it's time that women truly owned their superpowers and used their beauty and strength to change the world around them."- *Janelle Monáe*

My Android Crush…The Beautiful Janelle Monáe

Yes I am in love with *The Electric Lady*
And so what; I don't care if she's an android or a
human baby
She's the lady whose funky sound has got me
going crazy
Bringing out the best influence to my artistic side
I dreamed of the day of her being my *Cindi
Mayweather* and I'd be her *Anthony Greendown*

She's a *Q.U.E.E.N.* no doubt
And as this woman pass by me, it's all truth that
the booty don't lie
But her message through music is more what I'm
concerned about
Because her powers uplift me as they subside me
Lettin'Go my pain and hurt

Take us back to *Wondaland,* so she can finish her
letter ending it with *Sincerely Jane*
So we can recite sweet music together in
harmony as we walk down the *Neon Valley
Street*

Kaiserrific

Sharing this beautiful love *Locked Inside*
together in the city of *Metropolis*

Janelle has my love hanging on the *Tightrope*
I will travel to *Many Moons* just to see her
Walk through the *Cold War* to be beside her
'Cause being around this cover girl presence is
my greatest reason to *Smile*
I can't resist those *Dorothy Dandridge Eyes*
I am down with the android love in this woman
I'm all for her *Dance Apocalyptic* structure and
movement through time
Sharing a deep, great, and powerful love for her
in the *PrimeTime*

*Janelle, you are one of my greatest inspirations. I
don't know if you'll ever get to see this but if you
do, please know you have made a huge impact on
my collection of music. I love your work and
mission that allow young ladies to follow in the
footsteps of a great woman. I am forever a fan of
yours and will continue to support you and your
works. Thank you...*

*Being who you are Janelle Monáe is... WHAT I
LOVE ABOUT YOU*

Kaiserrific

What I Love About You...

Reason Number Seven

This section of the book is my way of saying thank you to every woman that I've either known, heard of, or has been inspired by. It's not enough words that I can say to express what I truly feel for each and every of them. Every one of these ladies played a major part in my life one way or another…in every part of me I want to say that I love and I thank them all.

Kaiserrific's Special Thank You

Each one of you are listed here for a reason,
Each one of you played a part sometime or a
season
My way of saying thank you to all you wonderful
women
Thanking you ladies for inspiring me through my
ups and downs
Lifting my hopes and dreams
Continuing to believe in me as I walk this
journey
Thank you all for being special women in my life
Inside my circle
Inside my world
Inside my life of Kaiserrific
I love you all very much and this is my thank
you…

Roslind Kaiser (*my mother*)
Annie Mae Kaiser (*my grandmother*)
Kathy Lynn-Gray
Coretta Scott King
Betty Shabazz
Ruby Dee
April Baker
Latrica Sunshyne Scott
Marshata Randall
Dorothy Dandridge

Kaiserrific

Harriet Tubman
Josephine Baker
Kim Kelly Hudson
Velma Harris-Walker
Jenell Spence
Marquita Jackson
Tammi Holland
Teaira Whitfield
Raquel Bennett-Jefferson
Oprah Winfrey
LaKenya Harrell
Arika Parr
Patrice Carter
Dominique Atkins
Janelle Monáe
Tammy Flowers
Beverly Davis
Lena Horne
Jill Scott
Ella Fitzgerald
Sojourner Truth
Rosa Parks
Denelle Fisher
Rosemary Adams
Olivia Kaiser (*my aunt*)
Evelyn Hudson (*my great-aunt*)
Evita Graham

Kaiserrific

Fior Baptiste
Debra FoFeet Warren
LaRisa Battle-Scales
Conita Harris
Jennifer Sutton
Katherine Jackson
Michelle Obama
Sharron Owens
Tanisha Robinson
April Simpson
Sherrita Allen
Natasha Grace Phillips
La Keisha Tunstall
La Treisha Tunstall
Valerie Gardner
Cassaundra Tomlin
Carla Hampton
Jean Pate
Terry McMillan
Anjanette Clark
Gloria Banks
Barbara Lyles-Moton
Courtney Luster
Elisabeth Forsythe
Erica Lucius
Bessie Smith
Heidi Calhoun

Kaiserrific

Nicole Humphries
Shannon Jones (*my cousin*)
Kim Edwards
Jo Lena Johnson
Shirley McReynolds
Journii Walker
Danette Beckum
LeSheila Sombright
Angela Crawford
Laqueta Hill
April Nolen
Susanna Soto-Thomas
Diana Ross
Patti LaBelle
Jackie Joyner-Kersey
Angela Davis
Nikki Giovanni
Lauryn Hill
Charisma Blue
Chanese Davis
Shantelya Bonds
Debbie Allen
Phylicia Rashād
Mahalia Jackson
Kennethia A. Miller
Lyric Expression
M'Reld Green

Kaiserrific

Gayla Carter
Ebony Kaiser (*my niece*)
Shawnyae Burnett
Chantell McCline
Nina Simone
Shante Duncan
Joanna Brown
Kelly Rowland
Rebecca Giles
Sandra Roberts
Callie Lampkin
Tareka Gaston
Benita Arceneaux
Rhonda Mayo
April Johnson
Theresa Ward
Joy Thorpe
Tiffany B
Devvine Franklin
Ashante' Spencer
Shirley Chisholm
Kristian Blackmon
Tamara King
Keshia Hopkins
Sharon Campbell
Alice Walker
Bridgette Broadnax Chandler

Kaiserrific

Zora Neale Hurston
Billie Holiday
Cassaundra Jones
Lorraine Hansberry
Rosie Clark (*my grandmother*)
Whoopi Goldberg
Amy Winehouse
Barbara Jordan
Janessa Morgan
Antoinette Jones
Dionne Stewart
Michelle Williams
LaVita Bell
Etta James
Michelle Moland
La Vonda Bell
KeErica Parker
Jazmene Kaiser (*my niece*)
Bella Words
Adrain Hemphill
Poetry Travis
Keeva Washington
Keya Harris
Bushra Muhammad
Aigner Martin
Jenifer Lewis
Afeni Shakur

Kaiserrific

Voletta Wallace
Bessie Coleman
Bessie Smith
Kimberly Richardson
Helen Griswold
Melonie Montgomery
Poetess Cynthia Sherrell
Kelley Jenkins
Debbie Conner
Raven-Symoné
KeKe Palmer
Queen Latifah
Mary McLeod Bethune
Ronda Ross (*my cousin*)
Christelle Ray
Tanisha McDonald
Shalonda Turner
Shelley Ajeedapoet Fowler
Evelyn Hudson (*my great-aunt*)
Kendra Bass
Seanée Robinson
Tosha LaRue
Robia IggNhyte
Favour Renae
Atara Estes
Karla Reed
Kyra Carothers

Kaiserrific

Teal Saunders
Tina O'Kelly
Jessica Hughes
Shamika Kaiser (*my niece*)
Arvella Bell
Angela Bassett
Beyoncé Knowles
Kerry Washington
Diahann Carroll
Monique Paige
Jada Pickett Smith
Alfre Woodard
Taraji P. Henson
Cicely Tyson
Cassandra Guyton
Monique Rainer
Hattie McDaniel
Rochelle Aytes
Tamala Jones
Karen White-Donaldson
Vanessa Williams
Viola Davis
Regina King
Gabrielle Union
Mable Clark (*my aunt*)
Terry Clark (*my aunt*)
Vivica A. Fox

Kaiserrific

Dun-Yal Rhone
Lisa Bonet
Tyra Banks
Beverly Johnson
Eva Marcille
Toccara Jones
Audra Bean
Debbie Conner
Madame C.J. Walker
Christina Parks
Talisha Harden
Marjorie Joyner
Annie Turbo Malone
Dr. Mae Jemison
Carla Jacks
Janelle Mack
Jessica Brown
Marian Anderson
Dawn Brown
LaShonda Williams
Ida B. Wells
Ruby Johnson
Brenda Hampton
Brenda Nash
Candice Young
Tiffany James-Robinson
Candice Bright

Kaiserrific

Beverly Forest
Ashley Boyce
Erica Roberson
Ashley Mc Larty
Aja Marie Brown
Ashley Hearod
Rhoda Pruitt
Shirley Ann Shepard-Adams
Ayanna Woods
Belle Nartley
Barbara Williams
Bernadette A. Williams
Chakita Carter
Chanel Thompson
Charisse Moore
Charlotte Small
Chasity VanHook Parker
Courtney Lowe
Angela Smith
Danielle Harlan Balabekyan
Danysha Kaiser (*my niece*)
Danielle Cooney
Danielle Wilson
Daphney Staten
Davina Eubanks
Devvine Franklin
Elisha Moaning

Kaiserrific

Erica Williams

Tricia Coleman

Eileen Doyle

Adrienne Jones

Sonya Wells

Gabrielle Buford

Ericka Galloway

Tiffany Kaiser (*my sister*)

Paris Kaiser (*my niece*)

Julia Griffin

Rhonda Lorthridge

Rachel Jones White

Janay Reynolds

LaParis Williams

LaToya Spence

LaKeya Green

Rosie Hill

Janice Stamps

Marquita Mosley

Ronda Goolsby

Yolunda Mopkins (*my cousin*)

Poetikk Justice

Melody Elliot

LaTori Turner

Denita Dyer

Trenisha Lavender

Tamika McClain

Kaiserrific

Kellie Williams-Box
Loyce Doss
Shantelya Brown
Karen Iona White
MiAhni Perry
Niecy Nash-Dixon
Shouna Reese
Kianna Hogan (*my niece*)
Angelete Thomas-Ashley
Kendra Williams
Nicole Chissem
Crystal Kaiser (*my niece*)
Nicole Harris
Dedra Woods
Bell Darris
Anita Fowler
Audrey Pearson
Hope Greene (*my niece*)
Cheron Brash Phillips
Loren Davis-Stroud
Keisha Ervin
Brenda Hampton
LaShonda Patten
Jennifer Lopez
Dione Sieber
Bernadette Williams
Elisabeth Forsythe

Kaiserrific

Sheila Riley
Kim Edwards
Levon Franklin
Juanita Moore
Tracee Clark
Alona Thompson
Destiny Kaiser (*my niece*)
Grace Jones
LaToya Jackson
Bianda Sombright
LaToyia Spann
Audra Bean
Chyna Holbrook
Ebony Anderson
Aigner Chambers
Yolanda Buchanan
Timeka Jones
Elizabeth Jefferies
Erika Hankins
Danielle Cooney
Annitra Jones
Erica Lamply (*my niece*)
Marquita Williams
Talisha Mallory
Apryl Barnes
Cierra Hall
Margaret Flack

Kaiserrific

Levada Barber
Riesha Hargrove
Sharon Merriweather
Ashlei Ainsworth
Carla Hendon-Harris
Kim Lambert
Alicia Lee
Leticia Rice
Tynia Brewer
LaTonya Fentress
Vivian Black
Erica A. Smith
Catherine Rose
Aimee Heydt
Ife Jacobs
Ebony Phillips
Arnette Johnson
Hillary Clinton
Evangelist Kasablia Ogletree
Jacqueline Garwood
Sherleta Perry
Hope Greene (*my niece*)
Kima Wooten
Dennoris Moore
Pamela Wooten
Alia Davis
Sarah "Saartjie" Baartman

Kaiserrific

Phyllis Wheatley
Tisha Campbell-Martin
Tichina Arnold
Gwendolyn Brooks
Terri Shedatruth Thurman
Susan Spit-Fire Lively
Surreal Sista
India Arie
Nicole Poeticone Nelson
Kels DK Franks
KaNikki Jakarta
Theresa Tha Songbird
Georgia Me
Rewop B
Pamela Wiley
Ruby Johnson
Joslyn Staples
LaVonda R. Staples
Jessica Jones
Brittany Williams
Shenitria Wiley
Torri Brown
Marquita Mullins-McDonald
India Garth
Truenessia Combs
Ashante' Spencer
Princess Uri Monigan Dukes

Kaiserrific

Montrice Williams
Neakisha White
Adrienne Ward
Shayla Jenkins
Leslie Wilkins
Sheena Houston
Yolanda Jones
Jasmyne Andrews
Erika Hankins
Corinna West
Jessica Givens
Shalane Scott
Leslie Chapple
Regina Pritchard
Shai Heat
Nakeisha Whitney
Camillya Blount
Christy Moss
Michelle Knighton
Amber Terry
Camille Morgan
Tamara Clark (*my cousin*)
Rhoda G. Rho
Kelly Price
Faith Evans
Ariel Sims
EnVogue

Kaiserrific

Amira Walker
Ivy Coleman
Chandra Jones
MC Lyte
Yolanda Friarson
Karyn White
Mariam Robinson
Freida Jones
Katrina Thomas
Eartha Kitt
Arica Rainey
Jerae Crawford
Katrina Jones
Monique Smith
Natasha (*Lady Ace*) Phillips
Aretha Franklin
Camille Cosby
Gladys Knight
Alicia Keys
Eve
Sherice M Ford-Brown
Iman
Lachoina Dickens
Maia Campbell
Monica Calhoun
Kelly Rowland
Rihanna

Kaiserrific

Betty White
Lou-Kendra Holloway
Nia Long
Yuoranda Walker
Sanaa Lathan
Niketa Feazell
Erica Johnson
Betty Wright
Adrienne Rainey
Roberta Flack
Marvina Tolliver
Cher
Brenda Davis
Katherine Dunham
Kairra Johnson
Niketta Dailey
Racheal Brown-Raymond
Ena McKee
Berakiah Boone
Teena Marie
Mariah Carey
Tanya Grayer (*cousin*)
Donna Summer
Aphro Ingenue
Toni Morrison
Janet Jackson
Whitney Houston

"Think like a queen. A queen is not afraid to fail. Failure is another steppingstone to greatness." - Oprah Winfrey

The Nubian Dynasty

Nubian queens this is what I love about you…

You all are incredible
Supreme goddesses to my eyes
Queens that I bow my head to serve
A Nubian movement that's influenced in more
ways than one
Ebony Princess that captures our hearts
The absolute gems to my world
I love you ladies of the light, brown, and
chocolate melanin skin tone
You ladies are the perfect reflection of myself
The very women that can define a man's true
love
I love being in your presence and that's what
matters
You all hold the key to my heart,
Because you beautiful goddesses are the joys to
my world
You al will always be the women that us men
appreciate
Whether you all are young or old
Black women you all are the dynasty that wears
the silver and gold
Thank You…

Kaiserrific

What I Love About You...

Reason Number Eight

Kaiserrific

I dedicate this poem to every woman in the world…

What I Love About You...
My appreciation for women

What I love about you,
Is the fact that I can wake up to a new day and
know you are in the world,
Knowing your presence in my life makes all a
great difference
And with you being in my life makes up the
completion of me …

What I love about you,
Is the fact that we can pass by each other and you
would smell so good to me,
Smelling so sweet to match with your soft hand
as it brushes up against mines from a simple
hello
Leaving me smiling making my day,
Feeling like the luckiest man in the world

What I love about you,
Is how you change my pain into happiness
One word (*your word*), one touch (*your touch*),
one smile (*your smile*) does so much
You are my rare cut diamond shaped inside my
rough

Kaiserrific

With you loving me, I could never get enough

What I love about you,
Is that you can wake up early at the crack of
dawn,
Get the kids up, ready and off to school
Go off to work as you deal with all the stresses
coming from the workforce
And come home after a long day to make dinner
and help the babies with their homework
And put the babies to sleep just before you get to
relax before you start the day over again
I love a good mom

What I love about you,
Is that you have enough in you to put up with our
bullshit
I know us men can take you ladies through hell
and back
And when we do act right; you continue to love
us,
Be in our corner when everyone else turned their
back on us,
Appreciate us with flaws and all…
You are our number one cheerleader giving that
extra boost of support

Kaiserrific

Thank you for being the woman that was needed
in our lives

What I love about you,
Is that you deal with so many issues and no one
wouldn't even know
Yet, you continue to walk with your head up high
Remain confident and proud as you make it
through the day
In the end you come out to be the survivor
And I love the survivor in you…

What I love about you,
Is that you were made from the love given in
heaven,
I love everything about you
Your contribution to the lives of men and
children
Your contribution to our history of man and
woman as it continues
Your skill to turn every wrong situation around
and make it alright
Your hard work that you spend so much time,
Your unconditional dedication,
Your realness as it shows from your actions
And last but never least your unconditional love

I love you women and there are not enough things that we men can say about how we truly feel. You all are going be here as you were in the beginning of time to the end of time. I appreciate every last one of you as well as your achievements that were accomplished in your lifetime. You all are queens and I am one of the few that will forever be your servant. I bow my head now to be at your service.

About The Author

Kaiserrific was born and raised in St. Louis, Missouri. He has been writing since a young age. His many talents traces back to the mid 1990's to where it all began. But writing has been one of his many talents applies his best when creating such books to intrigue his readers for entertainment, informative, and inspiring purposes.

A 2013 National Poetry Awards nominee, Kaiserrific has been performing spoken word at numerous open mics and events in St. Louis since 2010. At the beginning of 2011 Kaiserrific pursue his career as a poet while writing his first book *Freedom Independent Revelation Emancipation* known to the world as *FIRE.* Released in February 2012 and was the beginning of a successful self published author.

In addition to the release of Kaiserrific's first book more books were published that gained their own popularity. In August of 2012 Kaiserrific published his third book *Derrty Lil' Sex Secretz: Based On True Events* a book of erotic short stories told by a group of men from St. Louis, Missouri. The stories focus around the men intimate encounters with women within their city. D.L.S.S. (as some call it) became his best selling and most popular book. From the success of the book lead Kaiserrific to be featured on a local television show in St. Louis. Plus gaining successful sales in both paperback and eBook format in certain parts of the United States and in other countries overseas.

In September of 2013 Kaiserrific released his sixth book *Derrty Lil' Sex Secretz II: N Between The Sheetz*. After the success of the first book, readers ask for him to come back with a whole new series of stories told by not only men but women too. The book features more mind blowing erotica along with a twist of events that occur in the new stories.

Kaiserrific is a father of one son Kemonee who is his truest inspiration. He spends his spare time in his writing studio creating, reading, writing, and coming up with new ideas for future projects.

In his efforts to promote Kaiserrific continues support all local artists from not only St. Louis but all over the world. Encouraging others to come out and support as well. He stated once for any artist to go onstage and share their talent with people is a beautiful thing. He hopes that you enjoy reading all of his books as much as he did writing them.

Find Kaiserrific On The Following Apps And Sites:

Facebook: Kaiserrific
Twitter: @KAISERRIFIC80
Instagram: Kaiserrific
Glide: Kaiserrific
You Tube: Kaiserrific
Reverbnation: Kaiserrific
SoundCloud: Kaiserrific
Website: www.kaiserrific.com
Email: kaiserrificforfans@yahoo.com

Kaiserrific

More books published by Kaiserrific

FIRE
Freedom Independent Revelation Emancipation
(ISBN: 978-1468125511)
Release date: February 23, 2012

EPISODES
Common Sense Messages Passages Reflections Thoughts
And All That Good Shit!
(ISBN: 978-1477666197)
Release date: June 20, 2012

DERRTY LIL' SEX SECRETZ
Based On True Events
(ISBN: 978-1478235859)
Release date: August 29, 2012

PASSION IS LOVE'S POETRY
(ISBN: 978-1477586167)
Release date: October 1, 2012

ANOTHER PART OF ME
The Writings of Christopher Kaiser
(ISBN: 978-1477586143)
Release date: November 29, 2012

DERRTY LIL' SEX SECRETZ II
N Between The Sheetz
(ISBN: 978-1482610529)
Release date: September 16, 2013

ANOTHER PART OF ME
The Writings of Kaiserrific
(ISBN: 978-1492744269)
Release date: October 5, 2013

IF YOU ENJOYED THIS BOOK, EMAIL KAISERRIFIC AT THE EMAIL ADDRESS BELOW. LET HIM KNOW WHAT YOU THINK OF THE BOOK.

ALSO INCLUDE ANY IDEAS OR SUGGESTIONS FOR HIS NEXT BOOK! YOUR INPUT IS ALWAYS IMPORTANT! HE THANKS YOU IN ADVANCE.

kaiserrificforfans@yahoo.com

IF YOU WOULD LIKE TO HAVE KAISERRIFIC PERFORM AT YOUR NEXT EVENT. PLEASE SEND YOUR INFORMATION TO EMAIL ADDRESS BELOW AND SOMEONE WILL RESPOND BACK.

BookBeArtistEnt@gmail.com

Made in the USA
Charleston, SC
05 March 2015